For Juliet
and for my mother and father

Contents

Personnel Management in the Hotel and Catering Industry

M. J. Boella MHCIMA, MIPM

WITHDRAWN

Barrie & Jenkins
a division of Communica-Europa N.V.

First published in 1974 by
BARRIE & JENKINS LTD,
24 Highbury Crescent, London N5 1RX

ISBN 0 214 20019 1

Printed in Great Britain by
Lowe & Brydone (Printers) Ltd, Thetford, Norfolk

List of Figures

Foreword

The hotel and catering industry must accept responsibility for the present manpower problems and be prepared to take the action that is needed to improve this situation in the future. The fact that this is one of the first books published in the United Kingdom on personnel management in the industry underlines how neglected this field has been in the past. It must be welcomed therefore as a creative and constructive approach to improving conditions of employment in the industry, which in turn will help to improve the status of the industry.

The book is concerned with the many aspects of personnel management which if adopted in a planned way will improve the effectiveness of staff and reduce labour turnover. Recruitment is put in its proper perspective. The effect of recruitment drives at home and overseas and instant image improvement will always be short lived unless this is supported by action in other fields.

Employment conditions within the industry have improved over the years but has it done more than keep up with the rate of improvement in other industries? The statistics published in the Department of Employment Gazette would suggest not. In the sixties there were signs that some of the major companies were adopting policies that would close the gap, policies suggested by professional personnel managers from other fields. This movement seems to have slowed down and the industry does not appear to have made the progress which was anticipated. This is a great tragedy as this development would have a spin-off effect on the whole industry, including the smaller units which are a major part of the industry.

More and more line managers and proprietors are however realising the need to adopt more imaginative personnel policies and this book not only provides a guide on how to do this but will also serve as a reference book in putting the policies into effect. Most specialist jargon has been avoided and this will be appreciated both by practitioners and students.

The author has drawn on his considerable and varied experience as a specialist in personnel management from both within and without the industry. This gives the reader the benefit that the practices have been tried in our own field but also serves to remind the reader that he can and must learn from other industries who are competing in the same labour market.

M. A. Nightingale, FHCIMA, *Secretary,*
Hotel, Catering and Institutional Management Association
January 1974

Preface

The idea of writing this book first came to me about ten years ago when, as a very inexperienced personnel officer with one of the country's largest hotel and catering organisations, I was unable to find a concise book which dealt with both the 'nuts and bolts' and the more important concepts of personnel management and which could be applied readily to the hotel and catering industry.

Since that time, although many more books of a general nature on personnel management have been written still nothing covering the subject with particular application to the hotel and catering industry has appeared. This is in spite of the fact that over a million people find full or part time employment in the industry's various sectors, and in spite of the fact that the Commission on Industrial Relations (no doubt promoted by the industry's doubtful labour relations reputation) has subjected the industry to no fewer than three separate reports.

Within these past ten years the industry has seen tremendous changes, the most important probably being the emergence of several major companies in the United Kingdom which now rank amongst the world's largest hotel and catering undertakings. At an industry level considerable efforts from some sections to improve the industry's expertise have resulted in the establishment of the Hotel and Catering Industry Training Board, and a National Economic Development Committee for the industry. In addition the British Hotel, Restaurants and Caterers Association (BHRCA) and the Hotel, Catering and Institutional Management Association (HCIMA) both came into existence as a result of the merging of several smaller bodies with the result that the industry is now beginning to present a more united front in trade, professional and educational matters.

Considerable progress has been made within the educational field too with over 10,000 students now following various courses, including university degree courses, leading to careers in the industry.

In spite of these developments and the efforts of some employers' and managers' associations such as the Hotel and Catering Personnel Managers Association (HCPMA) the industry is currently faced with an ever increasing staff problem.

In writing this book, therefore, I hope to make some contribution to improving the industry's standards of personnel management by indicating what I believe to be some of the more common short-comings with suggestions for improvements which may result in more people coming into the industry in return for rewarding and satisfying jobs and careers. As a consequence I believe that the industry will be able to play an even more important part in the economy of the nation.

I have two main readers in mind – the busy practising manager, and also the future manager – the hotel and catering student. In particular I hope that certain chapters such as those dealing with job descriptions, recruitment, advertising, staff selection and remuneration will be of value to all those managers and executives responsible for managing hotels, restaurants, public houses, and the many sectors of industrial and institutional catering. I hope also that the book will prove of value to those many managers who, without any training or preparation, find themselves suddenly appointed staff or personnel officer (in one of its many different guises). I hope that it will also prove useful to all those students following courses (such as the OND, HND, HCIMA membership, City and Guilds 353 and university degree courses) which lead on to supervisory and management positions.

Some of the more formal techniques I describe here are applicable mainly to larger organisations, to which the majority of graduates will gravitate early on in their careers. I hope however that the proprietors and managers of smaller undertakings will not feel that the underlying principles do not apply equally to them – because the only differences should be of degree and detail. The principles of sound personnel management apply equally to all organisations whether small or large.

In writing a book of this nature, which draws upon my experience and knowledge gained during the past twenty years there must be many people who have contributed in some way to the contents to whom I am grateful. In particular I would like to thank those who I believe contributed significantly. These are my ex colleagues at Price Waterhouse Associates and my fellow directors of HCS (Management Consultants) Ltd., who over the last two years have had to act as my personal 'sounding board'. Then I must thank Miles Quest, Editor of *Catering Times,* for giving me the encouragement to write this book and for permission to reproduce from articles written by me for his paper. I would also like to thank Alfie Forte of Fortes Autogrills Ltd., Derek Gladwell and his staff at Sheffield Polytechnic, and John Fuller HCIMA President for reading my first draft and for their invaluable suggestions, also Des Floody, depot personnel manager of J. Sainsbury & Co. and Peter Coulson, Ll.B., for checking the chapter on law, also the libraries of the British Institute of Management, the British Association for Commercial and Industrial Education, the Institute of Personnel Management, the Hotel Catering and Institutional Management Association, and the Industrial Society, for their considerable assistance in providing me with a steady stream of books and articles.

Finally, I wish to thank my wife Juliet because without her continuous encouragement, comments and assistance, which included the typing of two drafts, this book would certainly not have been written.

Michael J. Boella
30 July 1973

1 A background to personnel management

Within the last few years the United Kingdom has seen many important developments and changes in society, the major one probably being the considerable improvement in the standard of living of the vast majority of working people. These improvements have come about as a result of many different factors including greater national productivity, the improved welfare state, more enlightened management and, last but by no means least, pressure from trade unions.

The contributions made by the hotel and catering industry to this general rise in standard of living are considerable and varied although it is only now that they are beginning to be recognised. Tourism, of which the hotel and catering industry is the principle element, is now claimed to be the country's fastest growing industry and also one of the leading earners of foreign currency. The fact that millions of people eat meals at or near their places of work or study, rather than at home, would not be possible without restaurants, cafés, public houses and 'in house' catering facilities. Furthermore the improved standard of living enjoyed by most people has resulted in many more ordinary people being able 'to enjoy a meal out' for pleasure rather than necessity, and in spite of some reports hospital patients, by and large, enjoy a better standard of food than ever before, thanks to a more efficient and professional body of catering officers.

Yet in spite of these improvements to the standard of living for the majority of the country's population, and the technical improve-

1

ments within the hotel and catering industry itself, the conditions of employment of large numbers of the industry's staff have not even kept pace with those enjoyed by working people elsewhere. Admittedly at the top of the scale craftsmen, such as chefs who are in short supply, can command very high incomes, but at the other end of the scale kitchen porters, for example, may be lucky to earn a third of what they could earn for broadly similar work in many factories and warehouses.

The reasons for the slow rate of improvement in the industry's conditions of employment are considerable including an understandable reluctance on the part of many proprietors and managers to be among the first to charge realistic prices for their services. The main reason however is probably that the trade union movement is almost non-existent in most sectors of the industry and the wages councils have certainly not been a substitute. As a result, for which many proprietors and managers are obviously grateful, the industry has not experienced those industrial relations problems suffered by many other industries. In spite of this the industry has its own less obvious but very costly labour problems, including a staggeringly high labour turnover rate and a dangerously high shortage of all categories of staff (estimated in 1973 at about 100,000), which the industry was unable to reduce substantially even when about one million were unemployed in this country. These problems have not gone unnoticed by the government who commissioned three separate reports to be produced by the Commission on Industrial Relations, with the industry's own little Neddy undertaking yet another.

It is, of course, to be expected that some aspects of working in the hotel and catering industry are unattractive. There are the intrinsic problems which are unavoidable such as having to work evenings, weekends and bank holidays. Other problems however can certainly be reduced or eliminated by determined management action. These problems include unnecessary 'split shift' working, staff reliance on tips, ignorance of methods of calculating pay and distributing service charges, and management's reluctance to 'involve' staff in matters that affect their working lives. All these difficulties were highlighted by the CIR reports and these together with problems of management attitudes are undoubtedly the causes of much of the industry's labour difficulties. Even today for example many employers and managers expect their ordinary employees to be dedicated to their jobs, to have a 'vocational' attitude to their work, to sacrifice leisure time for pay that is not high by most standards. These same employers and managers fail to recognise that their own motivation to work is usually completely different to that of their staff, and that work people throughout the community are becoming less work-orientated for various reasons. In fact employers in this industry must reconcile themselves rapidly to the fact that the majority of potential staff are no longer vocationally committed. Instead, staff expect competitive conditions of employment and leisure, and unless these are offered the industry will remain permanently under-staffed. It is interesting to note that the major sector in the industry, where there is the least, and in many cases no under-staffing, is the institutional and industrial catering sector where leisure time and other conditions are generally far more attractive than in the remainder of the industry and where, incidentally, trade unions are most influential.

MOTIVATION OF PEOPLE AT WORK

In order to understand recent developments and attitudes to work it is vital for managers and students of management to understand the background against which these developments are occurring and to appreciate the serious implication they have for this industry, which is, after all, one of the country's largest employers. To do so, it is necessary to look briefly at the findings of those who have studied the behaviour of people at work.

One of the problems in attempting such a task is the amount of published work available and also the wide variety of opinions. As a result only what are considered (by the author) to be the most important points have been selected. (Anyone wishing to study the subject further should refer to the reading list at the end of this chapter.)

The study of people at work falls within the province of the behavioural sciences which are concerned with studying the relationship between individuals, groups of individuals and their environment. The knowledge obtained can be used in two principal ways, namely to understand and predict changes and also to bring about changes. The fundamental conclusion to be drawn from the work of recent behavioural scientists, and Abraham Maslow in particular, is that man is a satisfaction seeking animal motivated firstly by his biological needs. Hotel and catering managers should be more conscious of the truth of this than most others. In addition, but unlike most other animals, once his biological needs are satisfied further needs emerge – mainly of a social nature. This manifests itself in the pursuit of power, status, security and other outward signs of 'success'. Most people are not conscious of these needs which drive or motivate them. If, however, management can recognise them they can take appropriate steps to ensure that these driving forces can be used to the advantage of both the organisation and the individual.

The first need, the need for bodily comfort is satisfied relatively simply by adequate meals and housing. The welfare state, recognising that the satisfaction of this need is essential to the survival of individuals and of society ensures by and large that no one needs to go without food and shelter. Individuals in our society therefore no longer accept that working merely for food and shelter is an end in itself. There are many cases where people are financially better off, unemployed rather than employed, and consequently they choose to remain unemployed. Most people expect much more from their employment than being able merely to purchase food and shelter.

Physical security is also these days very largely assured by the State. Regulations designed to protect the community and the individual from injury or disease penetrate every aspect of our daily lives ranging from traffic to hygiene regulations. Even after this, if someone does fall ill or suffer injury, the State cares for him so that he need not fear the financial consequences to the same extent that he may have done a few years ago or that he might do today in many other countries. Therefore, seeking employment with low physical risk or with benevolent employers is no longer as important as it may have been 100 or even fifty years ago. Consequently, because our biological needs are now largely guaranteed by the State they no longer provide the motivation that they once did. Instead, other and much more complex needs – the social needs – have emerged.

Satisfactory relationships with other people are among the highest of our needs. To work with and for people we get on with is something most of us like to do, and it is no doubt a major force attracting many people into the hotel catering industry. In looking at staff turnover it should be noted that the greatest numbers leave in the earliest days of employment – the period when relationships have not developed. On the other hand, one of the main reasons why people stay in their job, when all other conditions should encourage them to leave, is because of their relationship with those at work including colleagues, bosses, subordinates and customers.

In our society another aspect of our relationship with others which plays a significant part is our need for social acceptance. Frequently this depends on our job and our way of living. By certain indications society locates us on the social ladder but many people not content with their position attempt to move up. This is usually achieved by earning more money, obtaining a variety of other status symbols such as motor-cars, longer holidays, thicker carpet in the office, etc., or even by changing from one occupation or employer to another with a higher social standing. This fact unfortunately deters many people from working in the hotel and catering industry because many jobs, in spite of being highly skilled, are not awarded their due status by the community. It is within this field that the industry's trade and professional bodies need to do a great deal more work.

Next on the list comes the need to satisfy one's own ambitions and aspirations. This usually means making the maximum use of one's intellectual, social or manual skills. It may include the desire to be a company chairman or, more modestly, merely the wish to produce a satisfactory piece of workmanship. Today with the undoubted economic need for mass production and consequent simplification whether it be the production of 'in-flight' meals or motor-cars, man's need for this satisfaction is constantly neglected. It is one of the working man's strongest needs and one for which he often makes considerable sacrifices. People will put in long hours in difficult conditions even for low pay when job satisfaction is high.

Finally – having satisfied all these needs – security of their continuing satisfaction is itself another and, these days, a growing need. Mergers and acquisitions along with rationalisation now threaten many more people than ever before, and even those who a few years ago could feel secure no longer do so. Seeking this security now plays an important part in labour relations and many people leave insecure employment for what they believe to be secure employment. It is usually found that where job security is high, such as in banking or insurance, labour turnover is low – completely unlike the rate of labour turnover in the hotel and catering industry, where job tenure is notoriously precarious with many employers. Job security normally leads to a stable and skilled labour force with many of the consequent efficiencies.

When all these needs are satisfied an employee is more likely to offer stable and competent service, but, if any one of these needs remains unsatisfied, he will almost certainly behave in a variety of ways that are in most cases contrary to the business interest.

Firstly he may seek employment elsewhere which offers him more likelihood of a satisfying job. Secondly he may seek other compensations such as extra money or more time off. If he has leadership qualities he may become the focus for group, rather than individual, dissatisfaction or aspirations and this may lead him to play an active part in trade union affairs or other similar activities. Thirdly he may just opt out and seek his satisfaction outside work, for example, at home or in club activities. This last is unfortunately not so often the case, since evidence indicates that those who obtain most satisfaction at work also play the biggest part in social or community affairs. In between these three distinct patterns of behaviour there are many degrees that most managers will recognise including absenteeism, lateness, waste, pilferage and of course lack of cooperation or even sheer obstructionism.

MAN MANAGEMENT AND STYLES OF LEADERSHIP

Another finding of considerable importance, highlighted by Douglas McGregor in his book *The Human Side of Enterprise*, is that most people behave in the way expected of them and consequently 'live up' or 'down' to their superiors' expectations. Therefore the relationship between a man and his boss can be described as a dynamic one – the higher the expectations made (within reason) of an employee, the higher the performance, and consequently even higher expectations can and will be made of him and met by him in the future. In this industry unfortunately some managers expect the worst from all their subordinates and by making this apparent they inevitably get the worst results.

The 'style' of management is therefore of vital importance in an organisation because this determines to a large extent whether employees will get satisfaction from their jobs and whether managers will achieve their business objectives.

Although many different authorities have written on leadership styles and qualities, each with his own concepts and classifications, for the purpose of this book the two extremes, authoritarian and democratic, together with the 'laissez-faire' styles of management are to be looked at.

The 'authoritarian' manager generally manages by issuing orders and instructions leaving little or no opportunity for discussion or even explanation. Today, with strong pressures for more participation, this type of manager is finding life increasingly difficult.

Secondly there are the 'democratic' managers, who recognise that they are not only leading, but are also part of a team and that this requires the others in the team – the staff – to be involved in decisions through discussion and explanation. Evidence generally indicates that nowadays this style is the more successful.

Unfortunately some managers of the older 'authoritarian' school feel that to consult subordinates is a sign of weakness and that democratic management is a way of sharing, ducking or abdicating responsibility. It should be clear though that democratic management should in no way be abdication. The final decision and responsibility should remain the manager's. Democratic management is a recognition that most cooperation and the best results are achieved by pooling knowledge and experience and by involving people in the decisions that affect them.

The third manager, the 'laissez-faire' type, abdicates responsibility – leaving his staff to face the problems that are rightly the manager's. This fact was referred to in the CIR report on hotels and restaurants and it is evident that far too many hotel and catering managers consciously or unconsciously avoid the high-pressure points, such as the restaurants, kitchens or reception areas, during busy periods. The staff are left to face complaints from customers without the authority to rectify or overcome causes of disruption. Some major companies have recognised this problem and they attempt to overcome it by making managers' offices as small and uncomfortable as possible.

In considering these three main types of manager it must be recognised that there are many other types and variations of degree and that no individual type (apart from weak management) is necessarily right or wrong. Circumstances, and time in particular, can make a manager who would have been highly successful in one situation emerge a failure in another.

PERSONNEL POLICIES

The way an employer recognises the needs of his work people and the style of management he adopts are demonstrated largely by his personnel policies, written or implied. These may be highly formalised and inflexible, as is frequently the case in larger companies, or they may be informal, flexible and unfortunately inconsistent as with many smaller employers. Fundamentally, however, personnel policies should assist line managers to achieve their objectives in the most effective manner by providing conditions of employment that attract, retain and motivate the appropriate labour force. They assist management to find the best possible candidates and to provide training for the successful applicants. Effective personnel management requires an imaginative role in beating the competitors in the employment market to a fair share of the available labour. Consequently good personnel policies can make considerable contributions to the success of an undertaking,

Fig.1 The personnel function

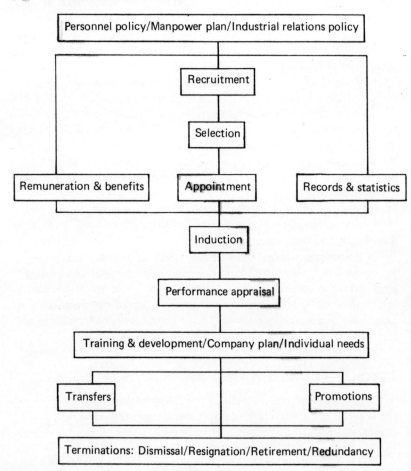

and although their efforts frequently cannot be measured accurately in monetary terms management should not be able to visualise doing its job effectively without the support of adequate personnel policies.

Figure 1 shows the main functions and responsibilities normally covered under personnel management.

FURTHER READING

Drake, R. I. and Smith, P. J., *Behavioural Science in Industry,* McGraw-Hill, London, 1973.

McGregor, Douglas, *The Human Side of Enterprise,* McGraw-Hill, New York, 1960.

2 Job description

Although the term *management* (in its abstract sense) has almost as many definitions as there are managers, it is generally understood to refer to the art or skill of achieving required results through the efforts of others. It is also generally held that people produce their best performances when they know clearly what is expected of them. Consequently if an undertaking's objectives are to be achieved it follows that all its managers and work people must know clearly the results expected of them. Such a statement of an organisation's expectations of its employees can be made either verbally or in writing, but experience proves that the written word is less likely to be misunderstood and that the need to think carefully before putting words to paper generally produces more logical and effective results than verbal statements.

Unfortunately, and often in the hotel and catering industry where jobs and conditions may not always be as attractive as one would hope, some employers avoid mentioning (if not actually concealing) the less pleasant aspects of the job, maintaining that if a man is applying for a particular job he should know what is involved. This thoughtless attitude to some extent accounts for the very large turnover of employees in their early days in new jobs.

It is for these reasons that clear, precise job descriptions should be given to everyone at work, because once a job is clearly described on paper there should be little room for subsequent misunderstandings. As a result a job should be performed more efficiently and labour turnover reduced

and labour turnover reduced

In some cases brief descriptions only may be sufficient, whereas in others quite detailed and complex documents are called for. The degree of detail needed in describing the various elements of a job varies from job to job and from organisation to organisation. There are however two main documents; job descriptions and job specifications. Job analysis is also sometimes considered to be a document describing a job in detail, but it is more correctly used when referring to the technique of examining jobs in depth. Job descriptions and job specifications are described below. In addition a brief description of Management by Objectives is included in this chapter

Fig.2   Job descriptions: the 'hub' of personnel management

because it describes a methodical and systematic approach to the description of jobs and the setting of objectives.

JOB DESCRIPTIONS

Job descriptions are a broad statement of the scope, purpose, duties and responsibilities involved in a job. Their main purposes are to :

1. Give employees an understanding of their jobs and standards of performance.
2. Clarify duties, responsibilities and authority in order to design the organisation structure.
3. Assist in assessing employees' performance.
4. Assist in the recruitment and placement of employees.
5. Assist in the induction of new employees.
6. Evaluate jobs for grading and salary administration.
7. Provide information for training and management development.

There are two distinct but equally important parts to the full description of jobs. The first is the statement of conditions for which employees contract to do work; some time ago in the United Kingdom it was recognised that the clear definition of conditions was not generally adequate, with the result that the Contracts of Employment Act became law in 1963. This Act with recent amendments requires that certain information regarding conditions of employment, such as hours of work and length of notice, be given to employees. This subject, together with other legal reasons for producing and issuing comprehensive job descriptions, will be dealt with in subsequent chapters.

The second part of describing jobs requires the provision of information to employees which specifies clearly what results are expected of them and indicates how their performance will be measured. Job descriptions should contain :

> Job title
> Department
> Scope
> Responsible to
> Responsible for (subordinates, equipment)
> Lateral communications
> Main responsibilities
> Limits of authority.

Figure 3 shows a typical job description for a chef and figure 4 shows one for a counter assistant.

Fig.3   Job description for a chef

Title:	Chef
Department:	Food & Beverage
Scope:	All hotel food preparation operations
Responsible to:	Food & Beverage Manager
Responsible for:	1. Personnel: all kitchen staff including kitchen manual staff 2. Equipment: all kitchen fixed & removable equipment & kitchen utensils
Lateral communication:	Restaurant Manager, Front Office Manager, Head Housekeeper
Main responsibilities:	The planning, organisation and supervision of food preparation in the hotel including: 1. Menu compilation according to agreed costed recipes 2. Purchasing of foodstuffs, kitchen materials and equipment from nominated suppliers within agreed budget levels 3. Portion and waste control 4. Control of labour & other variable costs within budget levels 5. Arrangement of staff rosters 6. Training of new staff 7. Hygiene and cleanliness 8. Fire precautions 9. Security of all kitchen supplies, equipment, utensils and silverware
Limit of authority:	1. Engagement and termination of all subordinates except chefs de partie 2. Right to suspend chefs de partie until circumstances can be reported to the Food & Beverages Manager

JOB SPECIFICATIONS

In many cases more detail than is normally contained in a brief job description may be necessary for a job to be performed satisfactorily. A detailed statement of the job may be required specifying the precise skills and knowledge needed to carry out the various component tasks of a job. This information may be contained in a document often referred to as a job specification.

Fig.5 Extracts from a job specification for a waitress

Duties	Knowledge	Skill	Social skills
1. Preparation			
1.3 Preparation of butter, cruets, and accompaniments	1. Correct accompaniments for the dishes on the day's menu	Operation of butter pat maker. Preparation of sauces, e.g. vinaigrette	
3. Service of customers			
3.3 Taking orders	1. Procedures for taking wine and food orders 2. Menu and dish composition 3. Procedure for taking requisitions to kitchen, bar dispense and cashier		1. Assisting customers with selection in order to maximise sales 2. Informing customers of composition of dishes
8. Wine dispense	Product knowledge 1. Suitable wines for dishes on the menu 2. Suitable galsses for different wines 3. Correct temperatures for red, white and rose	1. presenting bottle 2. opening bottle 3. pouring wine	1. Assisting customers with selection 2. Dealing with complaints
	Licensing law 1. Young persons 2. Drinking up time		1. Refusing service 2. Asking people to 'drink up'
11. Preparation for cleaners after last customers have left			
11.3 Stripping tables	1. Safe disposal of ash tray contents 2. Disposal of cutlery, crockery, linen, cruets		

Alternatively, the information may be contained in such documents as manuals of operation, operating instructions and the like. An extract from a job specification for a waitress is shown in figure 5.

MANAGEMENT BY OBJECTIVES (MbO)

Management by objectives is a fairly recent approach to management which, if operated effectively, influences all levels and activities of an organisation. It usually relies heavily on specially designed job descriptions and similar documents. MbO seeks to integrate all of an organisation's principal targets with the individual managers' own aspirations. By concept it is typical of a *democratic* style of management although, in practice, it is often introduced by other types of manager.

MbO requires the establishment of an undertaking's objectives, the development of plans to achieve these objectives, and the methods for monitoring progress. At the same time each manager must be personally involved in the preparation of his own department's targets and in the means of achieving these targets. Objectives should not be handed down by superior to subordinate, but should be agreed between the two after all factors have been considered.

The critical areas only of each manager's job are defined, the objectives where possible are quantified, the means of checking results, of identifying obstacles and of achieving objectives are developed. Planning and improvement goes on continuously through review meetings, being held at regular intervals between superiors and subordinates. The procedure is illustrated in figure 6 and an extract from a MbO job description is shown in figure 7.

PREPARATION OF JOB DESCRIPTIONS AND JOB SPECIFICATIONS

Some managers like to prepare job descriptions and other such documents with the employees concerned, and generally speaking this is by far the best approach. Frequently, however, this principle can only apply to supervisory and management grades because the jobs of operative grades are often so clearly defined that discussion, apart from explanation, would only raise hopes that would be disappointed when it became apparent that no changes were forthcoming. Furthermore it is not always possible to involve the employee concerned because the need for a job description often does not make itself apparent until a person has to be recruited.

The preparation of job specifications normally requires a more skilled approach than that needed for the preparation of job descriptions. The uses to which such documents are to be put should determine who prepares them. For example if job specifications are to be used for training purposes, they should be prepared by training specialists and the line management concerned. On the other hand if they are to be used as a basis for work measurement, work study specialists should work with line management.

Whatever the form the description of jobs takes, however, vague terms such as 'satisfactory levels of gross profit' should be avoided

Fig.6   Management by objectives

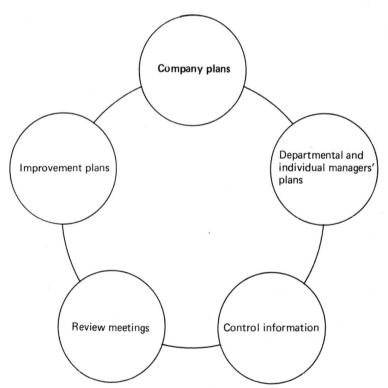

Fig.7 Management by objectives; example of performance standards and improvement plans

Manager, White Hart Restaurant: Objectives for six months ending 30 June

Key result area	Performance standard	Current level of achievement	Control information	Improvement target	Improvement plan
1 GROSS PROFIT					
(a) catering	58%	52%	monthly stocktake	achieve budget	Review selling and purchase prices, introduce more high yield dishes, by 30 April
(b) liquor	45%	42%	monthly stocktake	achieve budget	Alter sales mix, introduce premium priced beer, discontinue sale of cheaper draught beer
2 SALES VOLUME	£20,000	£22,000	takings sheets	increase to £28,000	Promote new private function room, spend £500 on promotion during first quarter
3 LABOUR	23%	26%	weekly wages sheet	reduce to budget, 23%	Increase staff only for booked functions, no more staff to be recruited except to replace those who leave

and, instead, actual quantities or levels should be specified, such as : 'a gross profit of fifty-eight per cent is to be obtained'. It is good practice also to incorporate budgets and forecasts into job descriptions as it sets specific and quantified targets. Additionally, documents such as manuals of operation or training booklets may be incorporated.

Because of the vital part played by job descriptions and specifications, particularly in such things as induction training, job evaluation and performance appraisal, their preparation should be monitored by one person or department to ensure consistency. They should be regularly updated and a copy held by the job holder, by his superior, sometimes by the superior's boss as well, and of course by the personnel department, where one exists.

Too many employers in this industry expect results without defining clearly what these should be or how they are to be achieved. Instead they expect employees to know intuitively what is wanted of them at the same time leaving them unsupervised and undirected for long periods. This lack of job descriptions results in new staff often being dissatisfied because the job is not as was described in the first place. Furthermore, lack of careful and methodical job description results in poor training so that service to the customer is frequently inconsistent and unsatisfactory. On the other hand employees' jobs could be made more easy, more satisfactory and the results of their work more predictable and efficient if their jobs were defined clearly.

FURTHER READING

Boydell, T. H., *A Guide to Job Analysis,* B.A.C.I.E., London, 1970.

Humble, J., *Management by Objectives in Action,* McGraw-Hill, London, 1970.

3 Recruitment

The hotel and catering industry has a notorious reputation for its exceedingly high labour turnover. In looking at some individual establishments there are cases where statistically it appears that the complete staff changes several times a year. Statistics of course can be misleading and closer examination will show that such high rates of turnover are confined to certain sectors only of the industry and to the more junior and less skilled employees. In spite of this, however, it must be recognised that the high turnover among employees, such as waiters, waitresses, bar staff and kitchen staff, is a very heavy drain on the time of the managers concerned, as they are called upon to recruit and train newcomers. Apart from this, the continuous fluctuations in standards of service cause irritation and dissatisfaction to customers which can only be damaging to the undertaking concerned.

By itself, good recruitment cannot overcome the problem of high labour turnover. This has to be tackled by keeping all conditions of employment under constant review and by making appropriate improvements to conditions as circumstances permit. The nature of the hotel and catering industry, however, is such that most people holding management or supervisory positions are going to be faced frequently with the need to recruit people to fill vacancies.

Recruitment is the art of attracting suitable applicants from whom the most suitable person may be selected. It depends upon adequate information being available including full details regard-

20

ing the conditions of employment and the job to be performed —
preferably in the form of a job description.

PERSONNEL SPECIFICATION

From these details a 'personnel specification' (sometimes called a
'man specification') can be prepared which is a description of the
type of person most likely to be able to carry out the job described
by the job description. The precise nature of a 'personnel specification' will depend upon the degree of sophistication or otherwise of
an organisation, but a comprehensive one should contain the
following :

1. Job title
2. Sex
3. Age range
4. Qualifications
5. Experience
6. Personal qualities including such things as adjustment,
   motivation and intelligence
7. Personal circumstances.

Point 6 is enlarged upon in the next chapter on selection methods.

From the job description in figure 3 therefore a 'personnel
specification' could be drawn up and might look something like
figure 8.

From the information contained in the job description and
personnel specification subsequent steps for recruitment can be
decided upon.

INTERNAL RECRUITMENT

The first step always in filling a position is to consider promoting
or transferring existing employees. Considerable dissatisfaction can
be caused by bringing newcomers in over the heads of present staff,
which is often done with the intention of causing as little disturbance
as possible to the organisation. Unfortunately, because the hopes of
some individuals in the organisation may be frustrated, they may
leave or behave in other unsatisfactory ways and the long term
effect is therefore far more damaging.

It is good management practice therefore for all vacancies in a
company, and particularly those that may be seen by existing

Fig.8   Personnel specification for a chef

1. **Job title:**   CHEF DE CUISINE

2. **Sex:**   Male

3. **Age range:**   28–50

4. **Qualifications:**
   (a) **educational:**   No formal requirements
   (b) **technical:**   City and Guilds of London 152
                               or Formal apprenticeship

5. **Experience to include:** (a) experience in all corners, but
                               in particular in the larder
                               (b) experience of controlling a
                               brigade of not less than five
                               (c) recent experience of good quality
                               a la carte service (up to 200 covers a day)

6. **Personal qualities:**   (a) able to control mixed staff of English,
                               Continental and Asian nationalities
                               (b) stable employment record (e.g. no more
                               than three jobs over the last ten years)
                               (c) above average intelligence

7. **Personal circumstances:** (a) able to work late (11 p.m.)
                               about three nights a week
                               (b) will have to live out

employees to be promotions, to be advertised internally on the staff notice board or by circulars. Circulating details to supervisors only is generally not satisfactory as some employees may fear that their supervisors will not put them forward for various reasons.

EXTERNAL RECRUITMENT

The next step, if no existing staff are suitable, is to go onto the labour market. This is where most problems arise and where most money and effort are wasted.

The numerous and varied means of recruitment include :
1. Newspapers : national, local and trade
2. Agencies, including the Department of Employment and the Youth Employment Offices
3. Executive selection and management consultants
4. Posters, e.g. on London Underground, in one's own premises, postcards in local Post Office windows
5. Colleges of Further Education
6. Armed forces.

The choice of media is critical to success and always depends on the type and level of vacancy. Generally speaking the higher level appointments will be advertised on a national basis and the lower levels will be advertised locally. For example, if a company is seeking to appoint an Area Manager for a group of hotels, the national press such as *The Daily Telegraph* or *The Sunday Times* could be used in conjunction with the trade press. On the other hand if a waitress is required, local employment agencies and the local press will probably be sufficient.

The likely mobility of applicants is of course vital and in this industry, where accommodation is provided, even less qualified categories of employees are often prepared to move large distances. Because of this the trade press can be used effectively. If, for example, a living-in bar cellarman is required, this can be advertised in a trade paper such as the *Caterer and Hotel Keeper* and the *Morning Advertiser* as well as in the local press, and through agencies. The table shown in figure 9 illustrates some suitable sources.

ADVERTISING

From figure 9 it is evident that a large part of any recruitment can be expected to rely on advertising and therefore, apart from the

Fig.9   Recruitment sources and media

Staff to be recruited	Sources and/or type of media	Examples
Senior executives e.g. Area Managers Regional Managers Hotel Managers	National press Trade press Consultants Agencies	*The Daily Telegraph* *Catering Times, Caterer and Hotelkeeper* Executive Selection Consultants, 'Head Hunters' Alfred Marks, Department of Employment
Departmental heads and managers of small units	Trade press Specialised sections of national press Agencies Armed services	*Catering Times, Caterer and Hotelkeeper* *The Daily Telegraph* Alfred Marks, Department of Employment Resettlement officers
Skilled employees e.g. cooks, waiters	Local press, including London evening papers and Common Market local press Agencies	*Evening Argus* *Evening News, Evening Standard* Alfred Marks, Department of Employment
Unskilled employees e.g. cleaners, porters, kitchen hands, part-timers	Local press Agencies Local colleges Notices & posters	*Daily Echo* Alfred Marks, Department of Employment Universities, Colleges of Technology (students) Displayed in Post Office windows or in own premises
Apprentices and trainees	Youth Employment Officers, Careers Masters	

choice of media, the drafting of advertisements is important. To recruit successfully these days, in the face of expert competition from other employers, it is no longer enough just to place an advertisement. It has to be a good advertisement. The rules for creating an effective advertisement are :

1. Be honest
2. Catch likely candidates' attention
3. Give clear, factual information including :
    a) locality
    b) job content
    c) prospects
    d) qualifications
    e) experience
    f) conditions of employment
    g) what action to take in order to apply
4. Keep the language simple if it is directed at unskilled applicants
5. Stimulate interest in the employer and promote his image, but remember that the priority is to fill a vacancy – not to advertise the establishment
6. Avoid box numbers
7. Avoid meaningless statements such as 'attractive wage' or 'salary according to qualifications'
8. Test the advertisement on others before finalising it
9. Stimulate the reader to act by telling him to call in, write or telephone.

Advertising a vacancy should be the method by which an employer communicates to potential employees that he is seeking to fill a vacancy. If the advertisement is loosely or vaguely worded it may encourage too many unsuitable applicants or, worse still, it may not attract the most suitable people.

There is an often quoted law of recruitment advertising that states that the ideal advertisement attracts only one applicant and that his application will be successful. This is obviously overstating the case but it does illustrate the need to think carefully about the choice and content of advertising. After all, the money wasted on ineffective advertising could well have been spent on new equipment, redecorations or even increases in salaries, and others in the organisation will not be slow to point this out.

The Chef's position described in figure 3 could be advertised in the form shown in figure 10. This illustrates an advertisement for a skilled person whereas advertising for unskilled people needs a different approach. For example, if advertising for a barmaid it

Fig.10   Display advertisement for a chef de cuisine

THE SPLENDIDE HOTEL
invites applications for the position of

Chef de Cuisine

vacancy larger than hotel name

The Splendide Hotel, part of an independent and progressive group, has an excellent reputation for its cuisine. It is situated on the sea front in Newtown and has two restaurants seating a total of 300 people, plus conference and function rooms able to cater for a further 300.

brief description of employer

The man appointed will be responsible to the Food and Beverage Manager for all kitchen operations including purchasing, gross profit control, menu compilation, and staffing. He will have a full-time staff of fifteen including porters.

job description

He will be aged 28–50 and he will have either served a recognised apprenticeship or will have obtained the City and Guilds of London 152. His experience must have been in top class establishments that enjoy a good reputation for their standards of food and service.

man required

The successful candidate will be paid a salary of not less than £3,000 p.a. for a five day week, including some late evenings. After the first year he will receive four weeks' holiday per annum, and will also qualify for the Company's pension scheme. Prospects for promotion within the company are excellent. This is a living out appointment.

main conditions of employment

Telephone, or write giving brief details of age, training and experience to

A. Smith, Food and Beverage Manager,

Splendide Hotel, Newtown, Newtownshire.
Tel.: Newtown (0021) 12345

how to apply

An example of an advertisement which sets out to create a good impression of the employer. It says a reasonable amount about the job and encourages people to apply in the simplest way.

may well be that the person appointed will need no experience, but some personal qualities instead, such as 'good appearance and personality'. For this reason the headline should be directed at *young ladies* not *barmaids* (see figure 11).

Fig. 11   Display advertisement for a barmaid

Local Press

THE SPLENDIDE HOTEL

situated in the centre of Newtown and catering for a busy
commercial trade requires

A SMART YOUNG LADY

to work as a part-time assistant in the cocktail bar. The successful
applicant aged 18–30 will assist the cocktail barman on Tuesday
to Saturday evenings each week. Once she has familiarised herself
with the work she will also stand in for him on Sunday evenings.
Hours will be 5.45 p.m. to 10.45 p.m. (The Hotel is on several
convenient bus routes which run up to about 11.00 p.m.)

No previous experience in bar work is required as training will be
given, but the ability to get on with people will be essentail. A
meal will be provided during the evening and the rate of pay will
be £1.75 per evening.

If you are interested telephone Mr A. Smith, Food & Beverage Manager.

**Splendide Hotel, Newtown,
Newtownshire.
Tel.: Newtown (0021) 12345**

There are three ways of inserting advertisements in newspapers: display, semi-display and classified. The two examples in figures 10 and 11 are 'display' and because they take up the most space and involve the most work they are the most expensive.

The second method is 'semi-display' which gives the advertiser some prominence in the classified section. Often this is all that is required to attract applicants. An example of semi-display is shown in figure 12.

Fig. 12   Semi-display advertisement for a school cook

NORTHERN SCHOOLS
BOARD

COOK
(Full-time or Part-time)

Applications are invited for the above
position in the Board's modern Head
Office Canteen in

New Road, York

Basic rate of pay will be 55p per hour.

The successful applicant will undertake general cooking in this modern
canteen.   Excellent conditions of
service are available.

Experience of large scale industrial
catering would be an advantage.
Interested applicants should write
quoting Reference No. 48 giving
details of age and experience to:

**The Director of Personnel,
Northern Schools Board,
New Road, York**

**by 20 March, 1974 or telephone
York 12345**

between 8.30 and 5 p.m.
Monday to Friday.

Classified advertising is the least expensive and usually the least
effective. This is because a large number of job advertisements are
lumped together and consequently are less likely to catch the
reader's eye. This is most likely to be the case when trying to recruit
unqualified part-timers, because these are often recruited from
normal readers who are not looking for jobs and consequently they
will not look up the classified columns. On the other hand, a good
display advertisement may well attract their attention and prompt
them to apply. Many girls, after all, have never thought of themselves working in a bar, but the advertisement in figure 9 would

Fig. 13   Classified advertisement for a cook

COOK 1, pay £21.57 and COOK II.
Pay £17.67 at 18, £19.64 at 19 or over
(pay includes pension contributions),
required at Post Office Staff Restaurant Telephone Exchange, 72 Fore
Street, London, EC2. Hours 8 a.m.
to 4.30 p.m. Monday to Friday.
Holidays with full pay, meals and
uniform provided, opportunity for
long term employment. Apply to:
MISS McGILL. TEL: 01-628 4791

probably prompt several to apply. Figure 13 shows a typical classified advertisement.

RECRUITMENT AGENCIES

In large organisations where recruitment costs run into thousands of pounds a year, it is advisable to retain a recruitment agency. Usually their services cost little as they receive a commission from the newspaper owners. Smaller firms, on the other hand, will not be able to offer recruitment agencies enough business for them to be interested, but in this case the newspapers themselves will always give advice and guidance.

WORD OF MOUTH

One particular method of recruitment has been purposely left until last because of the unique and important part it plays in recruitment. People in this industry know well the value of 'word of mouth' recommendation. Many highly successful hotels, restaurants and public houses do not need to spend a penny on attracting customers. Their reputation is enough. This applies equally to staff and there are many successful managers who never have to spend a penny to recruit new staff. Consciously or unconsciously, their existing employees recruit newcomers for them.

This method of recruitment is particularly good because of the two-way recommendation. Your existing employee is recommending you as a good employer and the applicant is being recommended as a suitable employee. Recognising the value of this method of recruitment some firms actually stimulate it by paying bonuses to employees who successfully introduce newcomers to the firm.

COSTS

Recruitment, like any other business activity, costs time and money. Most other business activities are measured in some way and standards or ratios are used to indicate the efficiency or otherwise of the activity.

This principle should apply equally to recruitment if it is a regular and substantial part of the running costs of the business. Where an agency is retained they will calculate the cost effectiveness of various media, but if an agency is not used this should be

Fig.14 Recruitment costs analysis

Media	Job	Cost	Numbers of applicants	Numbers interviewed	Cost per applicant	Number of successful applicants	Cost per successful applicant
Daily Globe	Chef	£120	8	5	£24 15	1	£120
Evening Star	Receptionist	£40	20	12	£2 2	4	£10
Evening Star	Waiter	£40	4	3	£13 10	2	£20
Blue Agency	Waiter	£70	7	6	£10 10	2	£35
Department of Employment	Porter	—	16	9	—	2	—

calculated internally. Figure 14 shows a simple form for the analysis of such costs.

Analyses can be much more complex but something along the lines of the form shown in figure 14 will prove sufficient for the average organisation to recognise which means of recruitment is the most effective and which involves the least interviewing, correspondence and other administration.

A manager, as was said earlier, achieves his results through the efforts of other people. Without the right people working for him he is unable to achieve his objectives and therefore it is vital that he spends time choosing the right people. Recruitment is not a chore to be squeezed into the 'normal' working day; it is a vital part of that working day because if it is done properly most of the other tasks become easier.

(Organisations that can be of assistance in recruiting staff are shown in Appendix 1.)

FURTHER READING

Denerley, R. A. and Plumbley, P. R., *Recruitment and Selection in a Full Employment Economy,* Institute of Personnel Management, London, 1968.

Ungerson, B. (Ed.), *A Recruitment Handbook,* Gower Press, London, 1970.

4 Selection

One of a manager's major responsibilities is to implement action but to do this he has to receive and interpret information in order to arrive at conclusions that will lead to the right action. The further up the hierarchy of management a man moves the more he exercises the skills of judgement and the less he carries out routine and supervisory tasks. In fact a senior manager's job is normally devoted almost entirely to making decisions that implement action and to designing systems that enable better decisions to be made. The skill of personnel selection is concerned entirely with this same process. In filling a vacancy a manager obtains information, sorts it, compares it, makes conclusions and implements action. This is illustrated in figure 1.

A manager will use the selection procedure normally for three different occasions:

1. To choose the most suitable person from several applicants to fill one vacancy.

2. To choose the right job from several for an applicant or several applicants.

3. Where there is only one applicant for a vacancy to decide whether or not to appoint the person and, if so, to know his strength and weaknesses so that additional supervision or appropriate training can be given, or so that the job can be modified.

In order to do this he should go through the procedure (described

32

Fig.15 The selection procedure simplified

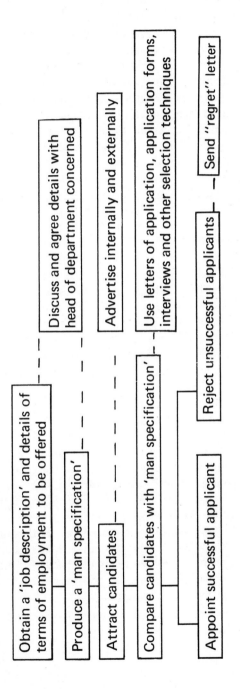

Obtain a 'job description' and details of terms of employment to be offered

Discuss and agree details with head of department concerned

Produce a 'man specification'

Attract candidates

Advertise internally and externally

Compare candidates with 'man specification'

Use letters of application, application forms, interviews and other selection techniques

Reject unsuccessful applicants

Send "regret" letter

Appoint successful applicant

in Chapters 2 and 3) which requires a comprehensive job description and man specification to be prepared. Correct advertising will have attracted candidates and it is then the manager's job to ensure that information is obtained from candidates in a way that enables a comparison to be made with the personnel specification. From this procedure the most suitable applicant will emerge.

To assist in selection there are a variety of tools available to the personnel manager including letters of application, application forms, interviews, group selection procedures and a range of tests sometimes referred to as psychological tests.

Selection procedures attempt to predict as accurately as possible a man's likely performance in a particular job or, where there are several vacancies, the job in which he is most likely to be successful. Most selection methods are of a 'historical' nature, that is they base their predictions on a man's past. However, most people accept that, economic and human considerations apart, the best method would be to employ a person for a period of time and then, if he proves satisfactory, to offer him the job. This is obviously not a practical method, although 'trial periods' are used both consciously and unconsciously in most industries. Selection procedures, instead, need to be designed in order to elicit the most useful and appropriate information in the most economic way.

In attempting to assess or to measure a person's suitability for a job it is important to know what characteristics are to be measured. The range and descriptions of these characteristics can be vast and in many cases almost meaningless. Some interview assessment forms contain a long list of items including charm, punctuality, honesty, integrity, ability, etc. Many of these are supposed to be assessed (or guessed at) at an interview.

Most characteristics or patterns of behaviour, however, can be grouped under several broad headings and two methods of assessment in particular are of interest. The National Institute of Industrial Psychology has a system that uses seven broad headings and J. Munro Fraser's plan uses five. Both systems are excellent but the five point plan in particular merits examination here, due to its simplicity. The five point plan is a technique for measuring to what degree an individual possesses each of the following five points or groups of characteristics :

1. First impression and physical make up; appearance, expression and manner

2. Qualifications: educational, technical and professional
3. Adjustment: ability (or otherwise) to relate to circumstances and people
4. Motivation: drive, determination, needs
5. Brains and ability: mental and manual skills.

The degree to which each of these points is possessed by an individual is measured by reference to the normal curve of distribution. This is divided into five grades, A to E, and sub-divided into a total of twenty points. Figure 16 shows this. The average man falls into grade C around the middle of the curve. Those individuals possessing a higher than average degree of a particular point move into a higher grade and, conversely, those with less move down the scale. For example in the aspect headed 'Qualifications' which includes education, the average man scores around the ten mark because he was in the A or did well in the B stream of a secondary modern school. On the other hand someone who obtained three 'A' levels would score about sixteen, and someone who could not do better than average in the B stream in a secondary modern would probably score no more than seven. The same principle of measurement applies to all five points.

In producing a personnel specification, therefore, inclusion of these five aspects with indications of desirable grades would considerably improve the 'pen picture' of the man required. Then during the subsequent selection procedure, candidates should be assessed or measured in the same way, making it a simple task to identify the man with the nearest assessment to the personnel specification. He should be the most suitable of the candidates.

This necessarily brief description of the five point plan is intended to illustrate broadly one technique that enables a manager about to recruit an employee to indicate and grade specifically the personal characteristics needed to perform a job satisfactorily thus producing a detailed 'personnel specification'. Readers with a particular interest in interviewing should certainly read the two books mentioned at the end of this chapter.

The next step in the selection process is to obtain information from candidates so that this information may be compared with the personnel specification thus enabling the most suitable candidates to be identified. The least expensive way administratively would be to talk to someone on the telephone and to offer him the job at the end of the telephone conversation. It is surprising, in an industry that requires personal characteristics such as tidy appearance and

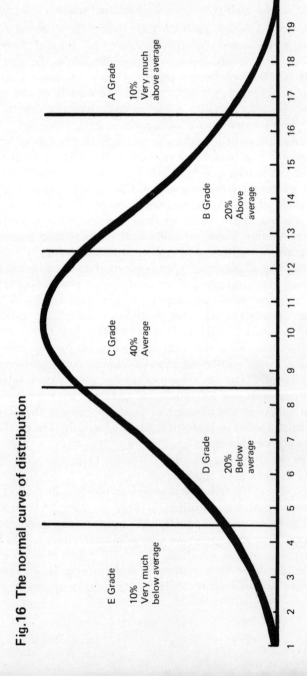

Fig.16 The normal curve of distribution

cleanliness, that anyone could be appointed in this way. But they still are. At the other end of the scale are group selection procedures that can last for thirty-six hours or more and involve the employer in very high selection costs. These procedures, however, are normally only used for management or trainee management appointments. Their success rate is usually considerably higher than less expensive methods. 'Success' in this context is measured by labour turnover figures, including 'survival rates' that show how long employees stay with an employer.

LETTER OF APPLICATION

Generally speaking it is not possible to use letters of application as a selection method any more than the telephone without the support of an interview. However, well-designed advertisements can ask applicants to give sufficient information from which some candidates can be invited for interview. A typical sentence at the end of an advertisement would read :

'Kindly write in giving full details including age, education, training, experience, and earnings to . . .'

To attempt to make an appointment purely on the strength of information contained in a letter is very risky and must be avoided.

APPLICATION FORMS

The application form is used primarily to gather together relevant details so that the selector has this information at his finger-tips and can make fair comparisons with the personnel specification and with other candidates' applications.

When designing an application form it is important to remember that it may have to serve several purposes, such as :

1. Deciding who to invite for an interview
2. Being used as an interview assessment form
3. Documenting employees and obtaining referees' names and addresses
4. Providing a reserve list of potential employees
5. Measuring the effectiveness of various recruitment media
6. Analysing the labour market.

The information required on an application form will, therefore, include some or all of the following :

1. Position applied for
2. Personal data : name, address, telephone number, age, sex, marital status, children, nationality
3. Education : schools, exams passed, and further education
4. Professional qualifications
5. Experience : jobs, duties, responsibilities, employers, earnings, reasons for leaving
6. Military experience : branch of the service, rank attained, experience
7. Personal circumstances : when available, prepared to travel or to move
8. Medical history
9. Interests, hobbies, sports, other activities.

The exact nature and extent of the information asked for will depend on the type of job and the employer's administrative requirements, but it should be confined as far as possible to information necessary for sound assessments to be made. It is not appropriate therefore for one 'blanket' type form to be used for all job categories. The type of form used for senior executives which asks about professional qualifications and total employment history would not be suitable for an unskilled worker, such as a chambermaid, where the last five years' work history may be quite sufficient.

THE INTERVIEW

The next step after candidates have completed and submitted their application forms, or discussed their qualifications on the telephone is to invite selected candidates in for interviews. The interview is the most commonly used method of selection. It is also the most abused because few people are trained in the skills of interviewing or take the trouble to develop these skills. Consequently many bad appointments are made because the candidate has not had the opportunity to show his paces, or because the interviewer could not interpret rightly the available information. It is not possible in this book to discuss interviewing in depth, but several excellent books have already been written on the subject (see *Further reading* at the end of this chapter). In conducting an interview, however, it is important to keep to a plan, and the simplest method is to follow chronological order – starting at childhood and working up to the present day. Questions normally

Fig.17 Application form for non-management positions

Splendide Hotel, Newtown,
Newtownshire.
Tel.: Newtown (0021) 12345

APPLICATION FORM
Job applied for

Surname *Capitals*   Full Christian names

Address

Dependants

Telephone No   Nationality

Are you a Registered Disabled Person? If yes please give your registration number

Have you ever been convicted of any criminal offence? If so please give details:

Education *Only complete this section if your full-time education ended less than 5 years ago*

School *last attended*   Exams passed

Details of Further education   Course and exams passed

Other training courses including HCITB courses

Have you been previously employed by this Company? YES/NO If yes please give dates
and position held

Date available   How did you learn of this vacancy?

Details of previous employment — last three positions. If this covers a period of less than 5 years
give details of other positions held

Name and address of employer	Date		Position	Wage	Reason for leaving
	From	19..			
	To	19..			
	From	19..			
	To	19..			
	From	19..			
	To	19..			
	From	19..			
	To	19..			
	From	19..			
	To	19..			

I understand that incorrect or misleading information may render me liable to instant dismissal
and that any appointment is subject to satisfactory reference

Applicant's signature   Date

Fig.18 Application form for management positions

S *Splendide Hotel, Newtown,*
Newtownshire.
Tel.: Newtown (0021) 12345

CONFIDENTIAL   Reference

APPLICATION FORM

JOB APPLIED FOR

We realise that to complete this form will involve you in time and effort, but this will help us to be as
objective and accurate as possible in considering your application. Information will be treated confidentially
and no reference will be made to your present or past employers without your prior permission.

Surname   First names
Block letters please ise

Degrees, professional qualifications, etc
Please state dates obtained ied

Address

                                     Home telephone number
Place of birth   if convenient

Date of birth   Age

Height

Weight

Marital status   Ages of children, if any

EDUCATION
Schools attended   Dates   Exams passed   Year

Further Education: Full-time and part-time
College/University attended   Dates   Exams passed   Year

PRESENT/MOST RECENT APPOINTMENT

Name and address of employer

Nature of business

Title of appointment   Location   Date appointed

Current basic salary   Bonus   Fringe benefits
                                                    including pension,cars, etc.

Please outline your responsibilities, stating to whom you are responsible and who is responsible to you.

OTHER APPOINTMENTS commencing with the appointment before that described above.
Please explain any gaps in employment history.

Year and month from to	Name and address of employer and nature of employer's business	Position held	Reason for leaving	Salary and benefits Starting Leaving

MEDICAL HISTORY Please give details of any serious accidents, illnesses or disabilities:

Please set out any further information which you think should be taken into account in considering your application, including professional, trade or community activities.

How soon could you be free to take up a new appointment?

What salary do you expect to receive?

Signature   Date

become more searching as one approaches current or more recent experiences, and must therefore be designed to test fully a man's claimed level of competence.

If necessary make notes during an interview, but do explain to the candidate that this is necessary so that nothing of importance can be forgotten. The following *do's* and *don'ts* will be useful:

Do

1. Have a clear job description, personnel specification, details of conditions, and an interview plan that contains prepared technical questions
2. Use a quiet comfortable room
3. Suspend all phone calls and other interruptions
4. Introduce yourself, be natural and put the candidate at ease
5. Explain clearly the job, conditions of employment and prospects
6. Ask questions that begin with When, Where, Why, Who, What and How. This avoids receiving 'Yes' and 'No' as an answer and encourages the candidate to talk
7. Avoid asking unnecessary questions already answered on the application form
8. Listen and let the candidate talk freely, but at the same time guide and control the interview
9. Encourage the candidate to ask questions
10. Close the interview firmly and explain the next step in the procedure
11. Treat all candidates as though they are potential employees and customers
12. Write up your assessment immediately after each interview.

Don't

1. Keep the candidate waiting
2. Oversell the job
3. Conceal unpleasant facts about the job
4. Interrupt or rush the interview
5. Preach to the candidate
6. Read out to the candidate what is on the application form; he filled it in and knows it already
7. Ask questions that indicate the answer
8. Ask questions that only get Yes or No for an answer
9. Allow the first impression to influence the whole interview
10. Ask unnecessary personal questions

11. Raise hopes unnecessarily

12. Leave the candidate with a bad opinion of your organisation

13. Wait until the end of the day or even till the following day to write up your assessments.

One final rule and a useful one by which an interviewer's skill can be measured is to estimate the amount of time devoted by the interviewer to listening and to talking. Generally speaking the less the interviewer talks the better he is at formulating questions, listening and making the right assessment.

GROUP SELECTION PROCEDURES

These are specialised techniques and should always be conducted by people trained in their design, operation and interpretation. The purpose of a group selection procedure is to observe candidates' behaviour in a situation or in a variety of situations similar to those they would have to face in the organisation. A group selection procedure could include :

1. The analysis of problems with written and verbal reports
2. Group discussions and debates
3. Business games
4. Individual interviews
5. Tests
6. 'Informal' drinks and dinner.

Group selection procedures are normally used to predict behaviour or personality traits that are difficult to assess in an interview or from personal history. These traits may include leadership ability, persuasiveness, self-confidence, ability to stand up to pressure, mental flexibility.

PSYCHOLOGICAL TESTS

The testing of individuals in education, at work and in other aspects of our lives has been going on in various forms for many years. Its main industrial purpose is to help to predict future performance in particular fields by understanding individual and group behaviour. As with other selection procedures testing assists in identifying the most suitable person for a job, and in identifying the most suitable jobs for individuals.

Mosts tests can normally only be administered under the supervision of a trained person registered with the National Foundation for Educational Research.

The five main groups of psychological tests are :

1. *Intelligence (I.Q.) or learning ability tests* : These measure the extent of an individual's ability to learn in various situations and are commonly used to predict whether a person will be able to attain certain academic levels. The 11 + is a typical example and claims to identify those children who have the intellectual capability to cope with the demands made by a grammar school education.

2. *Attainment tests* These measure the degree to which a person has acquired knowledge or skill. A craft test such as the City and Guilds of London 151 Professional Cookery examination is typical. Applicants for jobs such as cashiers, book-keepers or other clerical staff could be given simple attainment tests which could easily be devised by supervisors along with a personnel or training specialist. But it is important, in designing such tests, to recognise that failure to do the test may not indicate total unsuitability, but only a need for training.

Many more skill or attainment tests could be used in this industry including these shown in figure 19.

3. *Aptitude tests* This group of tests identifies an individual's innate suitability for particular types of work and can indicate whether a man would be more suited to one type of work rather than another.

4. *Interest tests* These tests indicate broadly which type of work an individual would prefer such as : indoor, outdoor, computational, gregarious, individual, routine, creative.

It is important to stress that an interest in, or preference for, particular work need not indicate an aptitude for that work. However, where an aptitude for a certain type of work is supported by an interest in the same type of work the chances of that individual succeeding are much higher.

5. *Personality tests* These tests determine an individual's reactions to different situations from which general conclusions can be drawn regarding likely future behaviour. They are concerned mainly with measuring non-intellectual characteristics. In particular they attempt to measure how a person relates to the

Fig.19 Attainment tests - examples of uses

Example of category of Employee	Nature of test
Chefs and cooks	Demonstrate knowledge of recipes and practical skill in making up certain dishes
Waiters and waitresses	Demonstrate knowledge of recipes, the accompaniments for certain dishes, and the service of some complex dishes
Barmen and barmaids	Demonstrate knowledge of and ability to prepare certain of the more popular drinks
	Demonstrate the ability to compute the cost of rounds of drinks
Cashiers and receptionists	Demonstrate knowledge of some common reception routines, the ability to operate appropriate office machines and to compute typical cash transactions

world around him and they do this by measuring the degree to
which a person possesses certain personality traits that may
include such characteristics as drive, stability, persuasiveness,
self-confidence.

TEST BATTERIES

It will be clear that each of the groups of tests mentioned above
attempts to measure limited aspects of an individual. These are
intelligence, attainment, aptitude, interests and personality. Each
individual we employ, however, needs each of these qualities to a
greater or lesser degree and one type of test only may not do him
justice. As a result some selection specialists use a battery or variety
of tests that measure several of those aspects of a person that may
be considered of importance. Additionally a test battery may be
only part of an overall procedure incorporated, for example, into a
group selection procedure.

REFERENCES

It is important to remember that references are only as reliable as
the judgement of the person giving them, and because of the fear
some employers have of putting a bad or indifferent reference in
writing many written references are worthless. The best procedure
for obtaining references therefore, is to telephone referees and to
discuss a candidate's application on the telephone. This discussion
should be written up afterwards so that it can be put into the
person's file. Alternatively, a standard letter or questionnaire asking
previous employers to confirm certain details can be used, see figure
20.

References must only be sought after a man has been offered an
appointment subject to references, as he may not have informed
his current employer of his plans to move; unless of course he has
given specific permission for references to be applied for before
being offered an appointment.

Successful selection, that is, placing suitable people into the right
jobs, is vital to the prosperity of an organisation. But selection can
only be successful if it is carried out methodically, and this requires
a clear job description and personnel specification, plus a system
which ensures that the most suitable candidates are attracted and
identified. This will require well-designed advertisements and

Fig.20 A reference enquiry letter

Splendide Hotel, Newtown,
Newtownshire.
Tel.: Newtown (0021) 12345

Dear Sir,

We have received an application for employment from Mr   who says that he was employed by you. It would be very helpful to us if you could answer the questions at the bottom of this letter and return it to us in the enclosed pre-paid envelope. The information will of course be treated in the strictest confidence.

If at any time we can be of similar assistance please do not hesitate to contact us. We hope that this enquiry does not cause you too much inconvenience.

Yours faithfully,

Please delete one

Full name

Position held   CORRECT/INCORRECT

Dates employed from   to   CORRECT/INCORRECT

Reason for leaving   CORRECT/INCORRECT

Would you re-employ him if you had a suitable vacancy?   YES/NO

Would you prefer us to telephone you?   YES/NO

Would you care to add any comments regarding his suitability for the job applied for:

application forms that elicit appropriate information. Interviews and other selection techniques, as outlined above, will then have to be conducted enabling the assessor to predict as accurately as possible a candidate's performance if he were to be appointed. This will involve knowing which characteristics are desirable and it will also involve using techniques that identify or measure those same characteristics.

Although careful selection is more time-consuming than haphazard recruitment, the reduction in labour turnover it brings about, together with the consequent improvement in efficiency and customer satisfaction make it worthwhile.

FURTHER READING

Denerley, R. A. and Plumbley, P. R., *Recruitment and Selection in a Full Employment Economy,* Institute of Personnel Management, London, 1968.

Fraser, J. Munro, *Employment Interviewing,* Macdonald and Evans, London, 1966.

Sidney, E. and Brown, M., *The Skills of Interviewing,* Tavistock, London, 1961.

5 Appointment and induction

First impressions are often the most lasting impressions, and the first impressions formed by many employees upon starting employment with a new organisation are unfortunately not often good impressions. While they may not be false, the employee is not to know this.

The notoriously high labour turnover in the hotel and catering industry results to a great extent from the impressions received by new employees in their first few hours or days of work. New employees arriving to start work are in many cases thrust straight into the job without even a minimal introduction to the employer's methods and rules, let alone introductions to colleagues and management. The first hours and days are critical and if properly dealt with will create the right relationship that contributes to employees' staying with an employer.

The process of correctly inducting an employee starts with the formal offer of employment. In these days of competition for good employees it is necessary to act quickly, and a successful applicant should be told immediately that the employer wishes to make an offer. This should be done, if possible, at an interview (not at the selection interview) or by telephone so that agreement can be reached on the spot about details such as starting date, outstanding holiday arrangements, etc.

Fig.21 Example of a letter offering employment

Splendide Hotel, Newtown,
Newtownshire.
Tel.: Newtown (0021) 12345

29 September 1973

Dear Mr Cook,

This letter is to confirm the conversation that we had yesterday in which I was very pleased to tell you that your application for the position of Chef de Cuisine has been successful.

I should like to confirm that you will be commencing employment on Monday 4 February next and that the following are details of the conditions of employment that we agreed.

Your pay is at the rate of £2,800 per annum. All meals will be provided whilst on duty. The Company undertakes to ensure that any future changes in the agreed terms will be communicated to you in writing within one month of the change. You will be paid monthly in arrears.

Your normal hours of work are 45 over a 5½ day week. The actual hours will be agreed on a weekly basis with the food and beverage manager.

Your entitlement to holidays (excluding public holidays) and holiday pay (including accrued holiday pay on termination of employment) is 3 weeks per annum. Your holiday will fall within the period May 1 - September 30 each year, the actual period to be fixed in accordance with the rota drawn up by the hotel manager.

You are covered by the Company's sick pay and pension schemes, details of which are set out in the accompanying handbook.

You are entitled to receive one week's notice of termination during the first twelve weeks of employment thereafter you are entitled to receive one month's notice of termination increasing to two months' notice after 10 years' service. You are required to give the Company similar notice of termination.

NOTE
Under the Industrial Relations Act 1971 you have the following rights as between you and the company:

    to belong to a registered trade union of your choice;

    to choose not to belong to a registered trade union or unregistered organisation of workers or to any particular union or organisation;

    if you belong to a registered trade union, to take part in its activities at any appropriate time and to seek and hold office in it. 'Appropriate time' means a time outside working hours or a time within working hours that has been agreed by your Departmental supervisor.

If you have any grievance relating to your employment, you should raise it with your Departmental supervisor, either orally or in writing. If the matter is not settled at this level, you may pursue it through the company's grievance procedure, details of which are set out in the accompanying handbook.

This offer is subject to satisfactory references and a satisfactory medical report from the company's doctor.

A copy of this letter is attached for you to sign and return to me which I shall treat as both an acceptance of the offer and permission to write to your referees.

You will find attached a copy of the job description which we discussed at the interview and if you have any queries, do not hesitate to contact me. Could you kindly bring your Insurance Card and P45 with you.

In the meantime I should like to wish you every success and happiness with the Company and look forward to seeing you in my office at 9.30 am on 4 February.

Yours sincerely,

LETTER OF APPOINTMENT

A formal letter should then be sent off incorporating all conditions of employment and also the job description. An example of a typical letter of offer is shown in figure 21.

This letter satisfies several requirements :

1. It gives the new employee full details concerning the job and conditions.

2. If fulfils the requirements of the Contracts of Employment Act by giving the employee details of certain conditions of employment and obviates the need to do this within 13 weeks of his joining.

3. It demonstrates an efficient, business-like, and by its tone, human approach that should make the man feel he is joining a worthwhile organisation.

4. It obtains his written acceptance of the offer and also written permission to write off for references.

5. It tells him exactly when and where to come, and what to bring with him, on his starting day.

DOCUMENTATION

The next step is to arrange that when the employee arrives all documentation proceeds smoothly. This includes obtaining the Insurance card and P45 and, where the employee is to be paid through a bank, his bank's address. A personal file or dossier will have to be opened which will contain all relevant correspondence and documents including the application form and acceptance of offer, and in time a variety of other documents.

Ideally an engagement form should be completed to ensure that no documentation procedures are missed out. This could look like the one illustrated in figure 48 (Chapter 16) and would be produced with sufficient copies for each interested department, including the wages department.

INTRODUCTION TO COLLEAGUES, RULES, Etc.

The second part of inducting a new employee is concerned with ensuring that he knows and understands what is required of him in order to do his job satisfactorily. This includes telling him or preferably showing him the layout of the place of work, introducing him to colleagues and explaining to him the function of other relevant departments. It will also be necessary for him to know about house rules such as 'no drinking' and relevant laws such as licensing hours and 'no smoking' in food areas.

TRAINING NEEDS

The third aspect is concerned with determining the employee's ability to do the job itself effectively and this will depend upon a man's training and experience. No training may be needed, or merely working under close guidance and supervision for a few days may be adequate. On the other hand, detailed training may be required and this is often the case in larger organisations that are prepared to employ untrained people and have standard methods common to many branches.

INDUCTION CHECKLIST

Whatever the level of competence, however, it is advisable to use a checklist to ensure that an induction procedure deals adequately with all necessary aspects of induction. In this context it is important to remember that what may not appear important to the employer may be very important to employees. A checklist is illustrated in figure 22.

Where it is discovered that some items mentioned on the list are not provided for in an induction programme, the latter may need to be amended. At the same time this example of a checklist is not claimed to be complete and further items could be added to it.

METHODS OF INDUCTION

Precisely how one introduces or inducts new employees to an organisation depends on many factors such as the newcomer's experience and knowledge, and the type and level of job he is to undertake. Probably the simplest and most common method is a short discussion in a supervisor's office followed by informal chats. This may be quite practical where a person's boss is readily available. However unless a checklist is used many points may remain unclear for a considerable time.

Another method could be the 'sponsor' method in which a newcomer, after an initial talk with his own supervisor, is introduced

Fig.22 Check list for Induction Programmes

1. DOCUMENTATION are the following points covered?	Name	Address		Tel No.
	Next of kin	Name	Address	Tel No.
	National Insurance Card		P45	
	Bank address			

2. INFORMATION
Are the following departments informed?

Wages/Pensions/Insurance/Personnel/Training/etc.

3. TERMS OF EMPLOYMENT
Are the following explained and understood?

Hours of duty/Meal breaks/Days off/Method of calculating pay
Holiday arrangements/Sick leave/Pension scheme/Grievance procedures
Rights regarding Trade Unions and Staff Associations
Additional benefits such as Group Insurance rates or other discounts

4. HISTORY AND ORGANISATION
Are the following explained and understood?

Origin and development of the organisation
Present situation/Objectives

5. ESTABLISHMENT ORGANISATION
Are the following explained and understood?

Layout of establishment including toilets, showers, etc.
Names of relevant supervisors and colleagues

6. RULES & REGULATIONS
Are the following explained and understood?

(a) Statutory; licensing laws and hours, food hygiene,
    Innkeeper's liability Act, etc.
(b) Company rules; punctuality, drinking, smoking, appearance,
    personal business, use of employer's property, etc.

7. THE JOB
Are the following explained and understood?

Purpose/Methods/Training needs

to an established employee who will 'show him the ropes'. This should not be confused with 'sitting next to Nellie' which is concerned primarily with training and not induction. If this 'sponsor' technique is used, however, the sponsor should be carefully selected to ensure that he knows what his duties are and has the necessary knowledge to carry them out. These would include many of the items listed on the induction checklist. A copy of this list should be given to the sponsor who would return it to the newcomer's supervisor once everything had been completed. This might take as little as a few minutes, or could be spread over several days.

Finally some induction programmes make use of formal training techniques in class-room situations. This is normally only used by larger employers that can afford the facilities and these programmes, apart from the initial documentation, may include talks, discussions and films on the company's history, organisation, rules and regulations. In addition a large part of the programme may be devoted to job training.

The advantage of formal systems such as the 'sponsor' and the class-room methods is that because one person is clearly responsible for the induction of newcomers it will normally be organised and conducted properly.

Induction can be considerably simplified by the preparation of clear 'handouts' or manuals elaborating aspects of employment that may need some explanation. Pension schemes and grievance procedures for example are ideally explained in written form owing to the amount of detail involved. Many other subjects too can be included in manuals such as trade union or staff association agreements, suggestion schemes, holiday arrangements, sick leave and fringe benefits.

In the obviously human field of man management comparing human beings with machines should be avoided but in the use of induction a very useful parallel can be drawn. Time spent in carefully installing and running-in a new piece of machinery usually results in that machinery giving long reliable service. It is as well to remember that in this context most human beings behave in very much the same way as machines.

FURTHER READING

Marks, Winifred, *Induction – Acclimatising people to work,* Institute of Personnel Management, London, 1970.

Induction, Industrial Society, London, 1973.

6 Appraisal

The appraisal of people at work goes on continuously. Every time a supervisor issues a good word or a reprimand some form of appraisal has taken place. From time to time, however, it becomes necessary for a supervisor to get away from the hurly-burly of the work place and to examine objectively the performance of his subordinates. He needs to do this because the company should know the strengths and weaknesses of its employees and because employees need to know how they stand. The supervisor should examine each employee's performance against expectations and at the same time he should consider the man's potential as well. He should then decide what steps should be taken in both the employer's and the individual's best interests. This process has several titles but is commonly called 'performance appraisal' and should be an essential part of any worthwhile manpower policy.

The appraisal of employees has one overriding objective and that is to improve the performance of the organisation. This is achieved by :

1. Identifying both individual's and group weaknesses and strengths so that weaknesses can be corrected and strengths developed and built upon.

2. Identifying each individual's hopes and aspirations so that, where these do not conflict with the organisation's objectives, they can be satisfied. This is necessary because when most individuals' hopes and aspirations are frustrated for too long they

will begin consciously or unconsciously to work against the employer's interest.

From a properly conducted appraisal programme an employer should obtain the following :

1. An analysis of training needs which enables individual and group training programmes to be produced
2. A succession plan and management development programme that earmarks individuals for promotion and identifies their particular development needs
3. A reasonably objective basis for salary review.

The individual also benefits by knowing :

1. How he stands and what help is to be given to improve his performance
2. What his career prospects are. (It is advisable not to discuss salary increases during an appraisal interview as this may well reduce the objective note that has to be aimed for.)

There are three main steps in conducting appraisals correctly :

1. Having an up-to-date and objective job description, and performance targets
2. Comparing the man's performance with his job description and targets
3. Communicating and discussing the supervisor's and the man's views regarding the man's performance, and the recording of both the supervisor's and the subordinate's views.

Job descriptions have already been discussed in Chapter 2 and it now becomes apparent why they should contain as many objective, measurable items as possible. For example if the word 'satisfactory' is used superior and subordinate may interpret the word differently. On the other hand, if an objective term such as '60% gross profit' is used, neither person can dispute the interpretation of this figure so long as each is clear about what is included in the calculation. In comparing a man's performance with his job description, therefore, it is necessary to bring together as much relevant information as possible such as budgets, forecasts and other records.

THE APPRAISAL FORM

The type of form used to record the appraisal is incidental to the interview itself although a well designed form can help in preparing for and conducting the interview. In cases where the form itself is of more importance than the interview – which is unfortunately only too common – the approach to the management of people is likely to be mechanistic rather than human. It enables the employer to achieve some of his objectives without fully considering the individual's own needs and aspirations. The design of the form therefore should be dependent on the purposes of the appraisal, but should contain at least some of the following:

1. Personal details, e.g. name, length of service, job, etc.
2. Performance report covering:
   a) Knowledge
   b) Skill
   c) Application
   d) Initiative
   e) Expression, written and spoken
   f) Ability to plan and to organise
   g) Ability to work with others
   h) Ability to direct others
   i) Specific job targets or objectives and the measure of achievement;
3. Training needs in present job
4. Potential
5. Training or development needs if promotable
6. General salary recommendation
7. Employee's comments.

TYPES OF APPRAISAL SCHEME

Some schemes require the manager making the assessment to place ticks in graded boxes, or to award points, as he judges appropriate. These schemes are often known as 'merit rating' schemes. They are relatively easy to operate, but just how reliable or fair they are is very debatable. They are particularly difficult to use for the assessment of non-quantifiable factors such as personality traits.

In 'written assessment' schemes much greater importance is attached to a freely written report. These types of schemes have the advantage of encouraging the manager making the assessment to think broadly about his subordinates rather than limiting them to a form full of boxes.

There are systems that compromise between these two extreme

Fig.23 Example of an appraisal form

PERFORMANCE REVIEW: PART 1   CONFIDENTIAL

Name of employee   Job   Branch

Completed by   Name   Position

Overall assessment *Put tick in appropriate boxes*   Whichever grade you award please elaborate here
                                                       on this person's performance:

    Excellent ☐   Satisfactory ☐

    Good ☐   Poor ☐

Detailed assessment		Excellent	Good	Satisfactory	Poor	Remarks
For all staff	Technical competence					
	Application					
	Initiative					
	Relations with: Supervisor					
	Colleagues					
	Customers					
For supervisory staff	Ability to direct others					
	Planning and organising ability					
	Expression: Written					
	Oral					

PERFORMANCE REVIEW: PART II   CONFIDENTIAL

1.
Is this person promotable, and if so, what type of job would most suit his abilities and aspirations?

2.
List what training can be given, or other action taken, to assist in improving performance or
preparing for promotion

3.
What salary increase would you recommend? Give reasons

High ☐   Low ☐

Standard ☐   None ☐

4.
Have you discussed this appraisal with your subordinate? YES/NO

If no, why not?

If yes, what were his comments?

types and which ask the manager to fill in boxes and to write a broad statement as well. One such scheme is shown in figure 23.

Ideally a system of assessment should reduce the non-quantifiable to a minimum and should concentrate the assessment on objective criteria, so that facts rather than opinions are used as a basis for the report and interview. This is, of course, what a well conceived MbO system attempts to achieve.

THE APPRAISAL INTERVIEW

The next, and the most crucial, aspect of appraisal is the conduct of the interview itself. Some managers find that asking their subordinates to examine and complete an appraisal report themselves makes the situation easier. This is known as 'self-appraisal' and enables a supervisor to study beforehand a man's views concerning his own performance. This obviously means that the supervisor is better equipped to get the best results out of the interview as he knows where the man is likely to be most sensitive. At the same time if the man has identified known weaknesses himself the supervisor can concentrate on means of improvement and on the future without dwelling on shortcomings and the past.

Many managers, however, find this approach too liberal and prefer to maintain a more 'normal' superior/subordinate relationship. Unfortunately this can involve the manager in playing two roles – judge and counsellor. This is a difficult problem for many to overcome, but if the manager can concentrate on the 'counselling' aspect and the future rather than making judgements and considering the past, this problem can be overcome to some extent. The precise nature of each interview will depend on the employees concerned. There are three principal methods – tell, tell and sell, tell and listen.

As with selection interviewing, appraisal interviewing is a skilled technique and those responsible for conducting these interviews need training and practice along with the ability to examine and criticise their own performance. Here are some useful rules to follow :

Do

1.   Plan the interview by obtaining all necessary information and by giving the person to be interviewed prior notice of the interview and of its purpose.

2.   Remember that interviews are a means of two-way communication and that the best interviewers do little talking themselves.

3.   Suspend phone calls and other interruptions and allow plenty of time for the interview.

4.   Put the interviewee at ease and try to make the occasion an informal one. (For example, avoid having the desk in between.)

5.   Make the interviewee feel that the main purpose of the interview is to benefit him.

6.   Start by praising strong points. Remember that a person has his 'ego' and that any subsequent criticism will be rejected as unfair or even untrue unless the balance is maintained by acknowledging good points.

7.   Ask for the interviewee's reasons for any shortcomings and ask for his suggestions for improvement.

8.   Finish the interview firmly on a positive note reiterating what performance is expected and what assistance the employee can expect in the form of training or other help.

9.   Remember always that giving a man a poor appraisal can be a reflection on the manager's own ability.

Don't

1.   Rush the interview. It is one of the most important occasions in a man's working year.

2.   Prejudge the outcome of the interview and therefore don't finalise the form until afterwards.

3. Read out the printed form. Your appraisal should come over in your own words.

4. Preach or be pompous. This is an occasion to discuss how a person's performance can be improved with your help.

SMALL ORGANISATIONS

In the smallest organisations with no more than a few employees a formal approach will be unnecessary and could even disrupt some healthy superior/subordinate relationships. Even so those employees with potential and prospects should be told of this so that they are less likely, as a result, to go to another employer for advancement.

Appraisal is one of the most personal and potentially unsettling situations that occurs in a working person's life. It is, after all, an examination and judgement of his main role in life and consequently it can be very damaging to his ego. It must therefore be positive, constructive and helpful. It should not be an occasion for apportioning blame or responsibility for past shortcomings or failures. If these are discussed they should be used as examples to illustrate points from which both sides can learn in order to take steps to build for the future. Appraisal must be creative and must result in new objectives and in agreement on the means by which these objectives can be achieved.

FURTHER READING

Maier, Norman R. F., *The Appraisal Interview*, John Wiley, New York, 1958.

Scott, B. and Edwards, B., *Appraisal and Appraisal Interviewing*, Industrial Society, London, 1972.

7 Training

One of the features of working life today is that whatever training is obtained at the start, it will almost certainly become redundant or obsolete during the same working lifetime. The need to train, to acquire new knowledge and new skills has become an everyday aspect of each individual's working life. In some cases this may merely be an updating process, but in others it will require a complete change from one occupation to another.

Some jobs and whole industries will disappear and other will emerge. Fortunately for the hotel and catering industry there is no likelihood of the main services it provides becoming redundant in the immediate future. Jobs within the industry may change, but the industry itself should flourish.

The responsibility for ensuring that working people are equipped to cope with these changes is threefold. The State carries a part of the responsibility particularly in providing training for school-leavers and for those who need retraining owing to the decline of their own industries, nationally or regionally. This responsibility is discharged by the provision of a variety of training facilities ranging from technical colleges and training centres to numerous types of grant.

Employers too have their share of responsibilities and they discharge these by providing training intended to suit their individual needs, or by participating, as do many employers in the hotel and catering industry, in group schemes which generally provide a good standard of training quite economically. Some employers provide excellent training whereas others are quite content to recruit trained individuals from the labour market without putting any trained people into that market themselves. The Industrial Training Act of 1964 recognised this and attempted, and largely succeeded, to stimulate industrial training and to spread the burden over most employers.

The third part of the responsibility rests with individuals. No amount of training will be effective unless an individual wishes to make the most of what is available. The State and employers may provide the best of facilities, but it rests ultimately with the individual to make the most effective use of these facilities for his own benefit and for the benefit of the employer and the community.

Industrial training is concerned primarily with bridging the gap between individuals' and groups' actual performance and the performance required to achieve an undertaking's objectives. These objectives may include such things as expansion, increasing sales, increasing profitability and improving standards. On other occasions training may be needed merely to maintain one's position in the market. However, there are some useful signs, or symptoms, that may indicate a need for training and these include :

1. Failure to attain targets such as gross profit on food or liquor, turnover, net profit
2. Dissatisfied customers
3. Slow service
4. High labour turnover, low morale
5. Friction between departments such as restaurant and kitchen
6. High accident, breakage, wastage rates
7. Staff unable or unprepared to adapt to changes.

It is not suggested that training alone can solve all these problems. If a hotel or restaurant is badly planned or wrongly situated, no amount of training (apart from training the executive responsible) can rectify this. However, training can often provide the solution or part of the solution.

Training should also consciously try to help individuals to reach the limits of their own capabilities and realistic aspirations – so long as these do not conflict with organisational objectives.

There are three main components that an individual requires in order to do his job effectively. These components are knowledge, skills and attitudes. Each of these can be developed or improved upon (from the organisation's point of view) by effective training. Each component, however, needs a different training approach. Knowledge for example can be imparted by talks, lectures and films, but these techniques would prove almost valueless in imparting the second component, skill, such as handling a knife. In this case, practice is necessary. The third component, a man's set of attitudes, is the most difficult to impart or to change, even with soundly based training, and it requires deep understanding of human behaviour by those responsible for training. Training techniques in this field may include discussions, case studies and role playing.

However, in order to design effective training programmes the following principles must be known and understood :

1. Training can only be successful if it is recognised that learning is a voluntary process, that individuals must be keen to learn and consequently they must be properly motivated. For example, if trainee waiters are losing earnings in the form of tips in order to attend a course, they may well begrudge the time and therefore may be unwilling to participate actively.

2. People learn at different rates and, particularly in the case of adults, often start from different levels of knowledge and skill and with different motives and attitudes.

3. Learning is hindered by feelings of nervousness, fear, inferiority, and by lack of confidence.

4. Instruction must be given in short frequent sessions rather than in a few long stints. For example, if a trainee is being instructed in the use of kitchen knives, ten lessons lasting forty-five minutes are obviously far better than one lesson lasting seven and a half hours.

5. Trainees must play active roles – they must participate. Generally speaking lecturing puts the trainees into a passive role, whereas discussions or practical work give them active roles.

6. Training must make full use of all the senses, not just one, such as the sense of hearing.

7. Progress must be checked frequently.

8. Confidence has to be built up by praise, not broken down by reprimand.

9. Skills and knowledge are acquired in stages marked by periods of progress, 'standstill' and even a degeneration of the skill or knowledge so far acquired. Instructors must know of this

phenomenon ('the learning curve') as it can be a cause of disappointment and frustration for many trainees.

These principles of learning illustrate and emphasise that it is both difficult and wasteful to treat individuals as groups. So far as possible training needs to be tailored to suit individual needs. The techniques to be used depend on a variety of factors, including whether it is knowledge, skills or attitudes that are to be imparted and whether individuals or groups are to be trained. The two main approaches are 'on the job' training and 'off the job' training.

ON THE JOB TRAINING

In the hotel and catering industry much of the staff's work is performed in direct contact with customers. For this reason much of the training of new staff has to be performed 'on the job' so that experience of dealing with customers can be obtained. 'On the job' training therefore plays a vital part in the industry's approach to training. If handled correctly it can be very effective for the teaching of manual and social skills, but it requires that training objectives are clearly defined and that those responsible for instruction are proficient in training techniques. Unfortunately, newcomers are often attached to experienced workers who are not in any way equipped to train others. This is often referred to as 'sitting next to Nellie'. Apart from not having a suitable personality they may not even have been told what to instruct and what not to instruct. Instead, if experienced workers are to be entrusted with the training of newcomers they should be chosen because of their ability to deal sympathetically with trainees, because of their knowledge of the job itself. They should then be given appropriate instructor training before being asked to train newcomers. The progress of trainees should be checked from time to time by the person responsible for training. Responsibility for training should not be abdicated to the instructor. An example of an 'on the job' training programme for a cocktail barman is shown in figure 24.

Note that the programme in figure 24 is in progressive stages. It requires each phase to be completely covered before the next is started. In addition this particular programme is only a checklist and therefore presupposes that the instructor already has the detailed knowledge. Because of this in many cases it will be necessary to expand this type of list by specifying in a document such as a training manual exactly what has to be instructed under each heading.

Fig.24 Example of an 'on the job' training programme for a COCKTAIL BARMAN

1ST STAGE

1. Bar preparation and cleanliness	(a) Washing down of bar counter, bottle shelves (b) Polishing of mirrors, glass shelves (c) 'bottling up' (d) Use of counter towels, drip mats and trays (e) Preparation of accompaniments including lemon, olives, cherries (f) Use of beer dispense equipment
2. 'Cash'	(a) Price lists (b) Use of cash register (c) Cheques and credit cards (d) Charging to customer accounts (e) Computation of costs of rounds and change 'giving'
3. Main points of law	(a) Licensing hours and drinking up time (b) Hotel residents and guests (c) Adulteration (d) Weights and Measures Act
4. Service of simple orders	(a) Beers, wines by the glass (b) Spirits and vermouth with mixers (c) Use of accompaniments such as ice, lemon, cherries (d) Cigarettes, cigars

2ND STAGE

1. Bar preparation and cleanliness	(a) Requisitioning of stock (b) Cleaning of beer dispense equipment (c) Preparing weekly liquor and provisions order
2. 'Cash'	(a) Checking float (b) Changing till roll (c) 'Off sales'
3. Further law	(a) Betting and gaming (b) Young persons (c) Credit sales of intoxicating liquor
4. Service of simple mixed drinks	(a) Shandies (b) Gin and Italian, gin and French

3RD STAGE

1. Bar preparation and cleanliness	(a) Rectification of faults such as 'fobbing beer', jammed bottle disposal unit (b) Preparation for stock taking
2. 'Cash'	Cashing up
3. Service of all drinks contained in house list	(a) Knowledge of recipes (b) Use of shaker and mixing glass

OFF THE JOB TRAINING

This is the form of training that takes place away from the working situation. A variety of methods and techniques may be used but the particular choice will depend on what is to be imparted. The main methods are :

a) *Talks* are best used for imparting knowledge such as company history and policies, legal matters, regulations, recipes, and an outline of methods and procedures. In giving a talk progress must be checked frequently by use of questions and answers.

b) *Discussions* are best used to elaborate on and to consolidate what has been imparted by other techniques.

c) *Lectures* often mean little more than talking at trainees and are therefore to be avoided as there is usually little trainee participation.

d) *Case studies, projects, business games* are best used to illustrate and to consolidate principles of management such as planning, analytical techniques, etc.

e) *Role playing* is best used to develop social skills such as receiving guests, handling customer complaints, selling, interviewing or instructional techniques. Ideally this should be supported by tape recordings and even closed circuit television recordings, if possible.

f) *Films, charts, and other visual aids* should not normally be used as instructional techniques by themselves, but should support talks, discussions, case studies and role playing. Films, and film strips on a variety of hotel and catering subjects are obtainable from several training organisations. These are listed in Appendix 2.

g) *Programmed texts and teaching machines* have a considerable future because they satisfy most of the principles of learning (mentioned on pages 22 and 23). In addition they can be used by individuals at any convenient time – not requiring the presence of an instructor. They cannot, of course, be used to teach some things such as manual skills.

An example of a fairly typical 'off the job' programme for cooks
is shown in figure 25.

**Fig.25 Example of first day of an 'off the job' training
programme for cooks employed by a firm
with many establishments offering standardised service**

Time	Subject matter	Method of instruction
9.00/9.45	Company history Present organisation and objectives Personnel policies	Talk, discussion and film
9.45/10.30	Kitchen equipment; cleanliness, safety, uses	Demonstration and discussion
10.30/11.00	Hygiene	Film and discussion
11.00/11.15	Coffee	
11.15/12.00	Principles of cookery; boiling, roasting and grilling	Demonstration and discussion
12.00/1.00	Portioning, preparation and presentation	Demonstration and practical work
1.00/2.00	Lunch	
2.00/4.00	Practical cookery	Practical preparation of simple dishes
4.00/4.15	Tea	
4.15/5.00	Costing and portion control	Talk and discussion
5.00/6.00	Clearing up	

TRAINING NEEDS ANALYSIS

Having looked at what training attempts to do, at the main principles of learning and at the main techniques available, the next step is to consider the design of training programmes. This starts with an identification of training needs, sometimes referred to as a 'training needs analysis', which is conducted by the person responsible for training in consultation with line managements. It should attempt to identify those *problems and opportunities* that line management could solve and exploit with the assistance of appropriate training. It should be produced firstly by studying the training needs of individuals as identified in 'appraisal reports' and then by detailed discussions with the line managers, who completed these appraisals. It should not be a long-winded process. The individual's job description, his actual performance and his potential should be the basis for these discussions.

From the consolidation of individual training needs will emerge corporate training needs. Priorities will then have to be allocated to each of these needs. Some will be 'essential' and some 'desirable'. These priorities should be laid down by senior management and will consequently fit in with the undertaking's business objectives.

In the case of an industrial catering contractor or of a group of restaurants, for example, there may be plans to expand the number of units and in order to do this a variety of key staff for the new units will be needed over a given period of time. It will be important therefore to identify those people who can be transferred or promoted and the training that will be needed in order to prepare them. This may range from preparing some assistant managers for full management to preparing junior kitchen hands to take over some more skilled responsibilities such as cooking.

The question of having sufficient trained personnel to fit into expansion plans is a critical one to the successful growth of an organisation and it is one area where the training function together with effective recruitment can prove to be of considerable value to a company.

All training needs obviously do not emerge from the annual training needs analysis. They also arise from unexpected changes in trading conditions or business emphasis. For example, many restaurant operators do not pay sufficient attention to the profits that can be generated by liquor sales. In this case, if a company decides that sales of drinks are to be promoted, effective training of waiters and waitresses in product knowledge, service and selling techniques can play a big part in boosting sales and profits. Likewise, a brewery may change its emphasis from running tenanted houses to running managed houses. In this case it will have to recruit and train managers to run the public houses; it will also have to train district managers in the supervision of managed houses.

LINE MANAGEMENT SUPPORT

It is vital that line management is seen to support training by participating in it as far as possible because if all instruction is left to the training staff an undesirable gap can develop between line management and the 'Teachers'. The best way to overcome this is to ask line management such as unit and departmental managers and the most skilled operators such as chefs and wine-waiters to be trained to take some teaching sessions. This ensures that the instruction given is in line with working requirements and conditions, but, of more importance, it persuades line management that training personnel are working with and for line management.

The subject of training is very extensive and because of this in some cases it becomes an 'end' in itself rather than a means to an end. It is therefore vital for it to be seen in perspective.

Training is one of the tools of management that should be used to increase an employer's profitability. It enables the undertaking's goals to be achieved by properly equipping its personnel with the knowledge, skills and attitudes necessary to achieve those goals. But at the same time training should also enable individuals to achieve whatever realistic aspirations they have in their work by enabling them, through increased competence and confidence, to earn more and to gain promotion.

(Organisations that can be of assistance in the training field are listed in Appendix 2.)

FURTHER READING

Barber, J. W. (Ed.), *Industrial Training Handbook,* Iliffe, London, 1968.

Singer, Edwin J., and Ramsden, John, *The Practical Approach to Skills Analysis,* McGraw-Hill, London, 1969.

Training Your Staff, Industrial Society, London, 1972.

Training Your Supervisors, Industrial Society, London, 1970.

8 Management development

As we saw in the preceding chapter on training one of the main concerns of senior management is to improve continuously the performance of those employed in the undertaking. But it should go without saying that training can only be effective if the right people are available to be trained. The well-being of any undertaking depends upon its staff and in particular on its management. Senior managers, therefore, have a vital responsibility to ensure that suitable people are available and are being developed to succeed to management posts as they arise. This must always be a major organisational objective.

An organisation needs to plan for natural replacement caused by retirements, resignations, deaths, etc., and in addition it needs to ensure that sufficient competent management is available for expansion plans. However, in a healthy organisation these plans must also extend to satisfying an individual's reasonable aspirations. For example, if an employer stands in the way of an employee's trying to obtain a recognised qualification by not allowing adequate time off, the employee will almost certainly place his qualification before his job and will seek an employer who will assist him. Plans that only accommodate the employer's needs will result in dissatisfaction, frustration, low morale and high labour turnover.

The senior management of an organisation must therefore ensure that adequate plans and resources exist to recruit, motivate, train, develop, and retain its existing and future management. This is all

71

part of the management development role, but in this chapter only the planning of management succession and the development of individual management skills will be discussed. Other aspects of the full management development function such as recruitment, induction and appraisal has been dealt with in other chapters.

A SUCCESSION PLAN

This is produced simply by comparing future management require-ments with currently available management. In order to do this organisation charts should be drawn up which show the structure of the undertaking at the present time and at various future dates, for example, three months, one year, three years, five years. Each job shown should have two boxes immediately next to it or under it in which the names of suitable successors can be inserted. A

See Fig 3

Fig.26 A management succession or replacement form

Position	Present job holder	Most suitable replacement *Put present job in brackets*	Second recommendation *Put present job in brackets*
Hotel Manager (Splendide)	J. Jones	A. Smith (Food and Beverage Manager, Splendide)	R. Barker (Front Office Manager, Grand)

Remarks

Signed by   J. Jones   Date   20/1/74

Approved by   J. Walker   (Area manager)

Fig.27 A succession chart

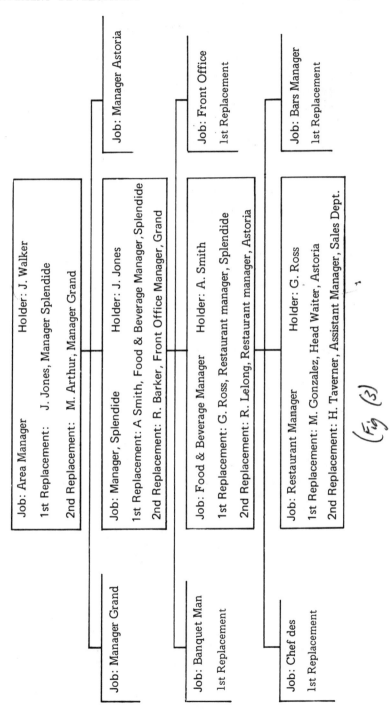

Job: Area Manager   Holder: J. Walker

1st Replacement: J. Jones, Manager Splendide

2nd Replacement: M. Arthur, Manager Grand

Job: Manager Astoria

Job: Manager Grand

Job: Manager, Splendide   Holder: J. Jones

1st Replacement: A Smith, Food & Beverage Manager, Splendide

2nd Replacement: R. Barker, Front Office Manager, Grand

Job: Front Office

1st Replacement

Job: Banquet Man

1st Replacement

Job: Food & Beverage Manager   Holder: A. Smith

1st Replacement: G. Ross, Restaurant manager, Splendide

2nd Replacement: R. Lelong, Restaurant manager, Astoria

Job: Bars Manager

1st Replacement

Job: Chef des

1st Replacement

Job: Restaurant Manager   Holder: G. Ross

1st Replacement: M. Gonzalez, Head Waiter, Astoria

2nd Replacement: H. Taverner, Assistant Manager, Sales Dept.

(Fig (3)

replacement form is shown in figure 26, and a succession chart in figure 27.

The names shown on figures 26 and 27 would result from discussions between the most appropriate levels of management and the personnel executive, using appraisal reports as a basis. This emphasises the need for a section on promotion potential to be included in the appraisal report.

So long as the basis for discussion is that replacement will be due to normal retirement, accident or the voluntary departure of the incumbent, the most appropriate levels of management to be involved in discussions will be:

1. The present holder of the job for which a replacement is being discussed
2. The present job holder's superior
3. The superiors of those proposed as replacements
4. A member of senior management fully aware of future plans
5. A personnel specialist (if one is employed).

In some cases one person will fulfil more than one of these roles. The final plan particularly for the more senior levels must carry the approval of senior management.

In order to identify likely successors in the first place it is usual to ask each member of management to nominate those he considers to be his most suitable successors. However, where this is done it must be recognised that there may be the danger of rigid departmental career paths, whereas in some cases, inter-departmental transfers and promotions will be more desirable in order to broaden experience.

In the largest organisations which are broken down into regional or functional operating companies the danger of 'sitting on' talent consciously or unconsciously has to be avoided. This can be achieved by all management above a certain level of seniority being dealt with as a 'group resource', in which case appraisals and other management development processes will be monitored by a central department.

DEVELOPMENT OF MANAGERS

Once a succession plan has been agreed, individual training and development programmes have to be designed. It is here that an understanding of how a manager acquires his knowledge, skills and attitudes is vital. People do not become managers in a classroom although they can acquire much of the necessary knowledge and basic skills there. Most of their expertise is obtained in the hard practice of managing people in the work place. A management development programme must therefore contain a balance of formal training and planned experience. It is not something that operates for one year only of a manager's life. It is up-dated every year and continues throughout a manager's working life. Over a period of years, therefore, a programme may include spells in line management and in various specialist departments. For example a young executive's first ten years with a company could be as shown in figure 28.

During this period the executive may also attend a dozen 'off the job' courses on such subjects as :

1. Supervisory skills
2. Budgetary control and forecasting
3. Techniques of instruction
4. Interviewing and selection techniques
5. Project planning
6. Finance for non-financial executives.

Whether these are internal or external courses depends on the needs of the organisation and the individual. Generally speaking, internal courses are more precisely designed to satisfy the needs of the organisation whereas external courses have to be broadly based to appeal to a wider market.

The value of external courses lies to a great extent in the opportunity to exchange views with managers from other organisations. But this only has value if those attending can bring about organisational changes. This prerogative normally lies only with more senior managers and therefore the value of external courses probably increases with the seniority of those attending (so long as it is geared to their needs).

The more junior people will be mainly concerned with acquiring knowledge and skills appropriate to their employer's needs and so long as the numbers justify it, this should be done internally which ensures that only relevant matter is covered.

TRAINEE MANAGEMENT COURSES

In this context the design of trainee managers' courses is critical. It is in the first months that the basis of knowledge, skills and, in particular, attitudes and values will be formed. During this period

Fig.28 Example of a career path for a young executive

Year	Approx. age	Position
1	21	Trainee management programme, various departments and establishments
2 3	22 23	Junior supervisory position, e.g. assistant manager of a hotel or restaurant
4	24	Specialised function, e.g. new projects department, sales office, training department
5 6	25 26	Line manager, e.g. unit manager, food and beverage manager
7	27	Specialist function, e.g. sales manager, training officer
8 9	28 29	Assistant to area manager
10	30	Line manager, e.g. manager of medium to large unit, area manager

however, unless worthwhile targets are set and some experience of supervision is obtained, most trainees will feel frustrated. For this reason there are many critics and opponents of the traditional 'Cook's tour' involving spells of training in the most important departments. In some cases this criticism is well deserved because no objectives are laid down and the trainees are merely used as cheap labour.

However, in order to be a successful manager, knowledge and experience of certain departments are vital and the well designed 'Cook's tour' serves this purpose; at the same time objectives must be agreed with departmental supervisors and trainees must be given their training objectives in written form. They should not move from one department to the next until departmental training objectives have been attained. Trainees should maintain training logs or diaries and in addition they should be given projects which should be completed by the end of training. Regular progress interviews should be held to ensure that the trainees' training objectives are being achieved.

In considering an individual's development programme, which is up-dated and modified year by year, it is vital to examine both his 'strengths' and 'weaknesses' remembering that they may well be strengths and weaknesses only so far as the employer is concerned. In another type of organisation the same characteristics may be seen in a completely different light. Ideally the weaknesses should be corrected and the strengths built upon. However, this will not always be possible because some 'weaknesses' may not be merely lack of knowledge or skill but of a 'personality' nature and these are often very difficult to correct even if it were desirable in the individual's interest to do so. For example a highly creative person may prefer to work as an individual. He may not enjoy or wish to work with others, nor to control them. His 'weakness' so far as the employer is concerned is that he cannot direct or lead others so the employer decides to give the man 'a spell managing others' to make him into an 'all-rounder'. In some cases this may work out, but in others it could have disastrous results, with the person concerned eventually leaving. Equally damaging, he could unsettle all his subordinates, who, it must be remembered, he may not have wanted to control in the first place.

It is vital, therefore, in designing management development programmes to recognise those 'weaknesses' that can be corrected and those that cannot. It is far better to build on strengths and to provide opportunities for these to be developed and exploited to the utmost, rather than to try to compensate for 'weaknesses' that may only be weaknesses in the employer's mind in any case.

FURTHER READING

Garforth, F. I. de la Pl., *Management Development,* Institute of Personnel Management, London, 1963.

Markwell, D. S. and Roberts, T. J., *Organisation of Management Development Programmes,* Gower Press, London, 1969.

9 Job evaluation

In many industrial disputes the levels of pay, the methods of calculating payment or the pay differentials existing between jobs are the underlying causes, but in the hotel and catering industry industrial disputes are rarely identified as such owing to the lack of organised labour. There are almost no strikes, so that what industrial action there is takes a different form showing itself in dismissals, dissatisfaction, resignations or 'walk outs', evidenced by the extraordinarily high labour turnover for which the hotel and catering industry is so notorious. In this industry wage levels are frequently determined by expediency rather than by any form of methodical approach. Newcomers are often recruited and paid more than existing staff doing the same job. Also many staff leave jobs because their employers refuse to grant increases even though the employers know that they will have to pay replacements more than the employees who have left.

A methodical, fair approach to the award of wages and salaries is vital to a harmonious relationship between employers and employees. In organisations employing over approximately one hundred people in about ten or more different jobs this can only be achieved if the relative value of each job is recognised and to do this a system of ranking jobs in order of importance needs to be used. It is important that a man such as a chef who has completed an apprenticeship and has acquired knowledge and skill should be paid more highly than a person whose job needs little knowledge or skill. It is simple to distinguish between jobs with skill and those without, but the problem arises when comparing jobs which are less easily differentiated, for example, when comparing those of a cook and a waiter. Both demand particular skills and knowledge but management has to decide whether to award more, and how much, to one rather than the other. A system of comparison that embraces all jobs within an enterprise needs to be adopted to ensure that wages are distributed fairly. Such a system, usually called 'job evaluation', provides a sound basis for comparisons to be made. Some systems attempt to be objective and analytical, whereas others are somewhat subjective but if managed properly they can be equally successful.

There are considerable benefits to be derived from introducing an effective job evaluation system and these include :

1. Less staff dissatisfaction caused by unfair pay and consequently lower labour turnover.

2. A logical basis for setting all wage levels, enabling the starting rate for newcomers and annual merit awards to be determined without upsetting existing employees.

3. A rational basis for differentials, that is the difference in pay for doing different jobs, making promotion and transfers easier.

4. Ease of producing labour cost forecasts. Where there is no methodical system it is more difficult to predict labour costs.

Symptoms that indicate a need for methodical job evaluation can include :

1. Employees leaving because wages are not awarded fairly and in particular because some newcomers earn more than long serving employees.

2. No formal periodic review of wages or salaries.

3. Difficulties, due to wage levels, in transferring and promoting employees.

4. A need to pay 'extras' or bonuses to get people to do what is, or should be, part of their normal job.

5. Some employees working excessive overtime.

In order to carry out effective job evaluation precise job descriptions and even job specifications are required because without these the comparisons of jobs becomes difficult, if not meaningless. Also, because comparisons of jobs are to be made the preparation of job descriptions must be standardised throughout the undertaking, and the actual evaluation should be conducted by one specialist or the

smallest possible number of people to ensure a consistent result.
The type of factors evaluated in each job may include :

1. *Knowledge.* This may be simple knowledge acquired in a
few days or at the other extreme may be acquired by several
years of study and application.

2. *Skill.* This refers mainly to manual skills. These may be
acquired within a very short period such as the skills needed to
operate a limited range of simple equipment, or they may take
many weeks, even months of practice such as typewriting, or the
varied skills needed by a competent cook.

3. *Responsibility.* This may be of the type where a person
makes important decisions that are not checked for a long period;
alternatively they may be simple decisions that are checked
immediately. This factor may include responsibility for people,
equipment, cash.

4. *Physical demands.* Some jobs are physically demanding
such as cooking, or they may make little physical demand such
as bookkeeping or typing.

5. *Mental demands.* All jobs, to a greater or lesser extent,
make demands on a person's mental abilities including the ability
to concentrate and to apply oneself. For example a senior receptionist's job will be much more demanding mentally than a
porter's.

6. *Social aptitudes.* Some jobs require more social skill than
others. A restaurant manager for example will require a high
degree of tact and patience, whereas a chef may require little or
no social skill.

7. *Ambient conditions.* This includes the amount of physical
and social inconveniences such as heat, long hours, and whether
sitting or standing. This may also take into account hazards such
as risk of burns and cuts.

These seven examples give a broad indication of the types of factors
considered. Others may be used and, in addition, a breakdown into
'sub-factors' may also be desirable. The main methods of evaluation
or how these factors may be measured, are shown in figure 29 (a
and b).

The most commonly used evaluation techniques however are :

Ranking. Jobs are put into an order of importance and then
divided into groups of similar rank.

Grading or classification. A grading framework is decided upon

Fig.29a Job Evaluation: non-analytical methods

Title	Broad description	Advantages	Disadvantages
RANKING	A simple method whereby the relative importance of the total job is assessed. Jobs are put in order of importance and may then be divided into groups	Very simple to use	Assessors need to know all jobs in some depth
GRADING OR CLASSIFICATION	A simple method in which a grading structure indicating relative job values is designed. Each job is then placed within the most appropriate grade	Very simple to use	Assessors need to know all jobs in some depth. Marginal jobs may be placed in higher or lower grade because system may not be sufficiently discriminating

Fig.29b Job Evaluation: analytical methods

Title	Broad description	Advantages	Disadvantages
POINTS ASSESSMENT	A commonly used and very acceptable method. Factors common to most jobs in the organisation are identified such as knowledge and responsibility. Maximum points are allocated to each factor weighted according to importance. Each job examined is broken into the various factors. Each factor is then awarded points between zero and the maximum. The total of points awarded will give the score for the job and thereby its standing relative to other jobs Bench mark jobs will be used to assist in allocating points	Simple to understand and operate	Takes longer to implement than 1 and 2. It can lead to considerable discussion on weighting of factors
FACTOR COMPARISON	Similar in some respects to points assessment but in some cases monetary values are used instead of points. Fewer factors, also, will normally be used than in points assessment Bench mark jobs will normally be used	Simple to operate once it has been designed	Difficult to arrive at monetary values
DIRECT CONSENSUS METHOD OR PAIRED COMPARISONS	A complex technique where evaluators representing all interested parties are asked to indicate which job of a pair or which factors within pairs of jobs they consider more important. The evaluators will probably deal with several or even many jobs. The paired comparisons of all evaluators may then be fed into a computer which will produce the ranking of all jobs considered	Reduces individual subjectivity to a minimum	Complex, usually needs a computer
TIME SPAN OF DISCRETION	This technique measures one factor only: the length of time in which an individual's work or decisions remain unchecked, e.g. a typist 4 hours, a managing director 4 years	Simple, once the concept has been fully understood	Sometimes difficult to determine true discretion span

Fig.30 A job grading or classification system (using the Institute of Administrative Management method)

Level Definition	Example of jobs
1. Very simple tasks of largely physical nature	Porter* Cleaner
2. Simple tasks carried out in accordance with a small number of clearly defined rules, and which can be carried out after a short period of training of up to 2-3 weeks. The work is checked and closely supervised	Chambermaid* Lift Attendant Counter Asst. Barmaid Hall Porter
3. Straight-forward tasks, but involving more complicated routines and requiring a degree of individual knowledge and alertness, as the work is subject to occasional check.	Commis Waiter* Clerk
4. Tasks calling for the independent arrangement of work and the exercise of some initiative, where little supervision is needed. Detailed familiarity with one or more branches of established procedure required	Receptionist* Waiter Cashier Store Keeper Florist
5. Routine work, but involving an individual degree of responsibility for answering non-routine queries and/or exercising some measure of control over a small group of staff	Head Waiter* Senior Receptionist Asst. Housekeeper
6. Non-routine work, involving co-ordination of several lower grade functions, possibly some measure of control over small group of staff. Also non-routine work involving recognised individual knowledge and some responsibility without follow-up	Head Housekeeper* Banqueting Manager Restaurant Manager
7. Work necessitating responsibility for sections involved on routine tasks and/or where there are also individual tasks to be undertaken, calling for specialist knowledge	Chef de Cuisine* Front Office Manager

* Bench mark jobs

and then jobs are put into the most appropriate grades. Figure 30 shows a typical approach, which is the system devised by the Institute of Administrative Management and demonstrates its application to jobs in the hotel and catering industry.

Points assessment. This method allocates points for each factor of a job. The points for all factors are added up and the total of points indicates the job's relative position in the job hierarchy.

The normal method of awarding points for each factor is to have a scale with 'bench mark' jobs on the scale. When evaluating a particular factor of a job it will be placed at or between what appear to be the most appropriate 'bench mark' job or jobs. For example in evaluating one factor such as knowledge the list of bench mark jobs is examined and the job being evaluated is then placed in the most appropriate position on the scale (see figure 31).

Fig.31 Example of Bench mark jobs

Points Bench mark jobs for *Maximum Points: 30*
KNOWLEDGE *Minimum Points: 0*

30   Hotel Manager

24   Front Office Manager

18   Restaurant Manager

12   Station Waiter

6   Hall Porter

In evaluating the knowledge required of a head waiter, for example, it would probably fall between the station waiter and the front office manager in figure 31, consequently being awarded somewhere between 5 and 10 points. The same procedure would then be adopted for all other factors to be evaluated. The bench mark jobs will not necessarily be the same for each factor.

After this has been done for all factors the points are totalled and the job grade should be determined by reference to a grade table such as shown in figure 32.

Fig.32 Example of a grade table

Grade	Points	Example of job
7	121-140	Chef de Cuisine
6	101-120	Restaurant Manager
5	81-100	Senior Receptionist
4	61-80	Waiter
3	41-60	Control Clerk
2	21-40	Hall Porter
1	0-20	Kitchen Porter

Figure 33 shows the technique applied to two jobs; a restaurant manager's and a commis waiter's. In this example the factors outlined on page 80 are used but in designing a scheme other factors entirely may be used.

After totalling the points a look at a grade table will indicate the grades of the two jobs. Refer back to figure 31.

The commis waiter's job therefore is a grade 3 and the front office manager's a grade 6.

This is a very simplified example of a points assessment system. Some systems may be much more complex than this, but no matter which technique is used, the principles of job evaluation are :

1. Job descriptions must be precise and up to date.
2. Because wages and salaries depend on the results evaluation must be scrupulously fair and consistent.
3. It is the job, not the job holder, which is being evaluated.

People at work measure their value to their employer, to a large extent by reference to the amount that they and their fellow workers

Fig.33 Example of a points assessment system showing the evaluation of two jobs

Factor	Maximum points	Example evaluation of two jobs Commis Waiter	Restaurant Manager
Knowledge	30	5	20
Skill	20	12	10
Responsibility	30	3	24
Physical demands	10	5	14
Mental demands	20	8	15
Social skills	20	12	16
Working conditions	10	5	3
Total	140	50	102

are paid. If, therefore, there appears to be unfairness or injustice in the methods or level of payment, employees will lose faith and confidence in their employer and will react accordingly. Arriving at a fair distribution of wages is not easy and only too often in the hotel and catering industry it is the result of expediency rather than methodical planning and application. It is vital, however, to recognise the relative importance of each job and, if they exist, to remove any causes that can lead to dissatisfaction. In order to do this it is vital, therefore, to adopt a methodical system of evaluating jobs so that wages and salaries appear to all to be fairly distributed.

(Organisations that can be of assistance in job evaluation are listed in Appendix 3.)

FURTHER READING

Job Evaluation and Merit Rating, Trades Union Congress, London, 1970.
Job Evaluation, Industrial Society, London, 1973.
Job Evaluation, Management Publications Ltd., London, 1970.

10 The administration of wages and salaries

The subject of earnings in the hotel and catering industry is a very contentious one owing to a variety of complications. Apart from the lack of method in setting basic rates, tipping, service charges and the provision of meals and living accommodation, all have to be taken into consideration. Within a single establishment it is quite possible to find a complete permutation of all the various benefits received by employees. Some live in and earn tips, some live out and do not earn tips, some are provided with meals and some are not. In addition, in the largest organisations some subsidiaries encourage tipping, whereas others do everything to eliminate it. This may be even further complicated by some area executives being provided with company cars and other benefits. On closer examination however it may well be found that these same executives are worse off (in cash and kind) than their own residential managers. Most of these anomalies however can be smoothed out by an effective salary administration system and this chapter therefore deals with the administration of wages and salaries using job evaluation as a basis.

It must be recognised that a major responsibility of managers is to decide how to distribute fairly among all employees the money set aside for payment of staff. This money may derive from normal revenue or may also come from retained service charges. Managers currently may decide by looking at what competitors are paying, what the wages council rate is, what has been historically the employer's practice and, in many cases, what is necessary to overcome the current crisis. The result is that considerable anomalies exist in many hotels, catering establishments and indeed in whole firms. As was said in the last chapter newcomers may be paid more than similar staff with long service and more senior staff may earn less than some juniors.

The exact policy to be adopted by an employer with regard to his wage and salary systems will depend to a great extent upon his business objectives, his personnel policies and his style of management. For example in organisations where labour turnover is not considered to be important there will probably be little method or formality in setting rates of pay. In other organisations, however, where it is recognised that a stable labour force is a valuable asset much more method will be applied to wage and salary matters.

Where there are many employees with differing levels of skills, fair salary administration will depend upon sound job evaluation which measures the relative importance to the organisation of different jobs. But after jobs have been evaluated, rates will have to be set for each grade to ensure that there are realistic differentials between grades so that more senior jobs and promotions are rewarded by worthwhile differences in earnings; promotion then becomes something to aim for. This is illustrated in figure 34.

Fig.34 Example of a grade and wage table

More senior jobs may be salaried and would appear on another table

Grade	Basic Wage	Example of job
4	£21 pw	Receptionist
3	£19 pw	Station Waiter
2	£17 pw	Chambermaid
1	£15 pw	Porter

Determining the rate for each job or for key jobs depends on many factors including the make up of the work force, statutory requirements, competitors' rates of pay, other industries' rates of pay, cost of living, and the location of the employer. Because of this, in order to establish or to maintain competitive rates of pay, it will be necessary to study advertisements in the press, to keep in touch with staff agencies and the local office of the department of employment, and with the local associations of hoteliers and caterers. In making decisions, as a result of this research, it is vital to ensure that all factors affecting rates of pay are taken into account, such as tips and service charges, actual hours worked, the provision or otherwise of meals and accommodation. Some employers with units in different regions may in addition require different rates or even entirely different structures for each branch or region.

INCREMENTS

In some situations it may be appropriate to provide merit and service increments and where this is done there should normally be overlaps between grades enabling someone in a low grade, but with long service or high merit, to earn more than someone in a high grade with short service. This recognises that a person's competence and value to an organisation usually increases with service, and because of this the increment is granted both as an increased share of his overall contribution and to encourage the employee to stay. (Figure 22 shows a table for such a scheme)

In the example shown in figure 22 an employee could anticipate, with satisfactory service, to move from the minimum to the maximum in a period of say five to seven years giving an average annual increase of about six to eight per cent. The exact rate would be determined by performance appraisals and by the employer's financial policy. The advantage of this system, if publicised, is that an employee knows what he can expect to earn by gaining promotion or by staying with his employer. In addition some employers have age-related scales or rates of pay, usually for employees up to about twenty-one years of age. Increases in these cases would normally be granted on each employee's birthday.

Starting wages or salaries offered to newcomers should not normally be more than twenty per cent above the minimum and this should only be permitted where appropriate experience in the

Fig.28 Example of an incremental pay system

Job grade	Example	Minimum	Maximum after 4 years
1	Cleaner	12	16.80
2	Lift Attendant	14	19.60
3	Clerk	16	22.40
4	Waiter	18	25.20
5	Senior Receptionist	20	28.00
6	Head Housekeeper	24	33.60
7	Chef	30	42.00

type of job justified it. Many trade unionists however are opposed
to incremental scales saying that every job should have a set rate
and that age and service are irrelevant if the job is performed
satisfactorily. Furthermore they claim that such systems can have
an adverse effect on staff turnover because management, in order
to keep payroll costs down, will encourage labour turnover, thus
retaining a high proportion of employees at the lower end of the
scales. This last argument however seems hardly tenable when they

industry's shortage of manpower is considered.

Reviews should take place regularly, for example annually, and should fit into the employer's budgetary and financial cycle. In seasonal establishments a review could take place towards the end of the season in order to retain those employees management want to keep.

Communicating details of any increases should be done as soon as possible after the decisions have been taken, but, as mentioned in the chapter on appraisals, they should not be part of any performance review or appraisal. Where a man is promoted, his increase should take place upon promotion. It should not normally be subject to trial periods as this can indicate meanness or, worse still, doubts about the man's ability to hold down the new job at the very time he needs his employer's fullest confidence. Nor should he have to wait for the annual review, because a man should be paid the rate for the job he is doing.

Apart from increases for merit, service and promotion, some systems also allow for cost of living increases to be made from time to time. These will probably be related to some government data such as the retail price index, but where these are granted it is important to bear in mind that they have little positive motivational effect – unlike a promotion or merit award. This is because they are usually granted to all employees without discriminating between the good and the not so good. On the other hand it is important to keep in mind that the absence of 'cost of living' increases may have a negative effect – that is the employees' relative level of earnings may fall and force them to seek employment with other more generous employers. It can be said that although 'cost of living' awards have little positive, motivational effect, their absence may have a negative effect such as a higher labour turnover.

As with all systems, there is no need to adhere inflexibly to the systems described – systems should be servants not masters. But experience shows that once a systematised salary structure is operational the whole question of pay becomes less contentious, and in particular where there are disputes or dissatisfactions over differentials management has a basis for dealing with these rationally.

Where systematic salary administration does not exist on the other hand there will almost certainly be anomalies, unfairness and, consequently, dissatisfaction. Staff will frequently leave, not because they are dissatisfied with their own level of pay, but because of some imagined or genuine grievance, such as learning that a newcomer is paid more than they are.

(Organisations that can be of assistance in the salary administration field are listed in Appendix 3.)

FURTHER READING

Salary Administration, Industrial Society, London, 1971.

Jaques, Elliott, *Equitable Payment,* Penguin, London, 1967.

11 Incentives

In addition to the normal wages or salaries which were looked at in the last chapter, it is common practice in many industries for some groups of employees to be able to augment their wages or salaries by earning additional payments in various forms. These payments are made largely to enable workers to participate personally in the success of the undertaking by rewarding individuals or groups for improved productivity of one kind or another.

There is a great deal of discussion about the merits or otherwise of incentive schemes. Some people argue that employees should be given an adequate wage or salary and, so long as other prospects are adequate such as the regular review of earnings and the likelihood of promotion, people will give what they consider to be a 'fair day's work'. The prospect of incentives will not spur them to continued greater efforts. In some types of work this may be true. For example in work of a highly creative nature the prospect of incentive payments will not stimulate greater creativity. There are others however who argue that incentives will certainly influence productivity saying, for example, that in a selling situation the prospects of earning commission will certainly stimulate greater 'selling' effort. It is also argued that because of the growing interdependence of working people they can no longer increase their own earnings without the involvement of their colleagues. In many cases nowadays this is true, but in this industry there are still many opportunities for individuals to increase considerably their earnings – particularly in the 'selling' areas such as waiting, bar work, hotel reception and function catering. Within the scope of this book it is not possible to consider the arguments for and against incentive schemes. There are unfortunately innumerable examples supporting both viewpoints. It is intended here to look at the main forms of incentives operated in the hotel and catering industry including tips, the 'tronc', service charges, bonuses and commissions.

In other industries other forms of incentive payments are also used. These include methods such as piece rates or measured day work, which are usually based on work study and measurement techniques, whereas those commonly used in the hotel and catering industry are more normally related to financial targets such as gross profits, turnover, and variable costs (i.e. gas, electricity). In some cases they may even be entirely discretionary.

Although *tipping* and the *tronc* were mentioned along with other forms of financial incentive it is probably better to think of them as part of normal earnings. Financial incentives are normally intended to stimulate and promote *extra* productivity whereas tips, the tronc and service charges are considered by employees as a matter of right and something without which they could not have a reasonable living standard.

Tipping is a form of payment that originated when many workers in the old inns were not employed by the innkeeper but were retained by guests to do particular jobs such as carrying bags, cleaning garments, etc. It also grew up in an age when it was normal to motivate people by fear. In the case of tipping the threat of a tip being withheld was used, and because there was probably no other income, the man's means of living was jeopardised. It is really an anachronism in this day and age and needs to be eliminated as rapidly as possible.

Service charges, on the other hand, are quite acceptable methods for an undertaking to employ to raise revenue, so long as the sum allowed for distribution to the work force is distributed on a fair basis. Additionally, where service charges are part of an employee's remuneration a minimum level should be specified so that a person can know how to regulate his affairs. For example if an employer knows that his waitresses normally earn £10 a week from the service charge and £13 per week in wages he could without much risk to himself offer a minimum guaranteed income of £20 per week. This guaranteed income could be paid weekly and the excess periodically, such as quarterly or half-yearly, thus spreading payment over good and bad spells of trade. Where a service charge is included in the bill, tipping should be actively discouraged and notices on bills, menus, brochures and in guest rooms should discourage guests from giving tips in addition to paying the service charge.

PRINCIPLES OF INCENTIVE SCHEMES

In designing an incentive scheme, whether for this industry or any other, there are several principles that should be adhered to for it to be effective in the long term. These are :

1. The undertaking's major business objectives should be promoted and their achievement assisted by incentive payments. These payments should enable individuals to identify with the success of the undertaking. For example, if food gross profit is vital the chef and maybe his staff as well should be rewarded for achieving gross profit targets. But only elements over which a man exerts control should be included. A chef for example has no control over the rent and rates, therefore there is no point in including these in a scheme for the chef.

2. When an incentive scheme is to be introduced *all* workers should be considered because of the effect the scheme may have on existing earnings differentials.

3. Payments should be related to results by comparing actual performance with forecasts, targets, standards, or budgets. This may be done individually or on a group basis.

4. Targets should be realistic, that is achievable with reasonable effort and agreed with the person or groups concerned.

5. Targets should be reviewed regularly, and at least annually, so that payments are something to be earned with effort rather than something which becomes a matter of right. They should also be reviewed if circumstances change considerably. For example, if a vast new office block opens next door to a snack bar, trade will probably increase considerably, through no effort of the manager. The turnover and other targets should, therefore, be reviewed at the same time bearing in mind that extra work will be created and that wages and salaries may have to be increased.

6. An incentive scheme should be simple and clearly understood by those within the scheme.

7. Payment of the incentive should be made as near as possible to the period in which it was earned. Long delays in payment cause irritation and reduce the incentive element.

8. All elements of a scheme and any rules should be objective. Management should not incorporate 'discretionary' rules such as 'management reserves the right to withhold payment without giving a reason'. Incentives, if earned, should be a matter of right, not for management to dispense on a discretionary basis, and the terms of the incentive scheme should become part of the 'Contract of Employment'.

Fig.36 Example of an individual incentive scheme (Chef)

1. Job   Chef

2. Commission   1% of all 'gross profit' (for this purpose
revenue less purchases and labour costs)
in excess of £500 per week,
after achieving the following targets

3. Targets   1. Purchases not to exceed 45% of revenue
2. Kitchen labour not to exceed 15% of revenue

4. Example of calculation

Period 7

Food cost	£1,500	(37.5%)	Revenue	£4,000
Labour cost	£550	(13.75%)		
	£2,050			
'Gross profit'	£1,950	(48.75%)		
	£4,000			£4,000

Gross profit £1,950 − £500 = £1,450 x $\frac{1}{100}$ =   £14.50

Commission to be   £14.50

ERRATA

~~re~~ 4 should appear on page 14.

„ 14: Amounts in the column headed 'Cost per applicant' should read: £15, £2, £10, £10.

„ 33: The figures in the column headed 'Restaurant Manager' should read: 18, 20, 24, 4, 15, 18, 3, 102.

„ 36 should appear on page 96.

Page 67: fourth line from the bottom 'pages 22 and 23' should read 'pages 64 and 65'.

Fig.4   Job description for a counter assistant

Title:	Counter Assistant
Department:	Depot General Canteen
Scope:	To assist in the preparation of meals, to keep the kitchen and dining areas in a clean and tidy state and to serve customers
Responsible to:	Assistant Manageress
Responsible for:	No subordinate staff
Lateral communication:	Cashier, cooks
Main responsibilities:	1. Prepare food stuffs according to directions 2. Clean and lay up canteen dining area 3. Stock up and replenish service points as necessary 4. Serve customers during service periods 5. Clear away used plates, utensils, trays, and wipe down tables and working surfaces during and after the service period 6. Clean and polish service equipment and kitchen areas after service periods 7. Comply with company standards and statutory hygiene regulations
Limits of authority:	No authority to authorise or make expenditure No authority over other staff

Fig.37 Example of a group incentive scheme

1. Department   Front Office

2. Commission   £5 for every 1% in excess of occupancy targets, distributed
                         to all front office staff pro rata to salaries

3. Target   85% occupancy

4. Example of calculation

Week 41

Actual occupancy 90.4% therefore 5.4 x £5 = £27 to be distributed

Salaries: Head Receptionist   £1600

   2 Senior Receptionists   @   £1200

   2 Cashier/Receptionists   @   £1000

     Total Salaries   £6000

$$\frac{£27 \text{ commission}}{£6000 \text{ salaries}} = 45\text{p per £ salary}$$

Therefore the following commissions will be paid

Head Receptionist   £1600 x 45p = £7.20

Senior Receptionists   £1200 x 45p = £5.40

Cashier/Receptionists   £1000 x 45p = £4.50

Incentives are normally used to stimulate performance and particularly to increase sales and control costs. Figures 36, 37 and 38 are included as examples.

Having looked at these examples, which are intended to illustrate principles only and which demonstrate that incentive schemes can be designed for many departments in an organisation, it is vital to bear in mind that their introduction may have undesirable consequences which could exclude their being used. For example, the chef may well place his commission above customer satisfaction and buy cheap materials or keep labour costs too low for efficient service. In the case of the receptionists they may overbook (more than is desirable) and consequently lose customers for the future. On the

Fig.38 Example of an individual incentive scheme (manager)

1. Job   Restaurant Manager

2. Commission   5% of net profit up to budget

                        10% of net profit between 101% and 130% of budget

                        20% of net profit in excess of 130% of budget

3. Target   £10,000 net profit

4. Example of calculation

Year ended 31 December 1973   Actual net profit = £14,000

Commission rate	Qualifying net profit	Commission
5%	£10,000	£500
10%	£ 3,000	£300
20%	£ 1,000	£200
TOTAL	£14,000	£1,000

In this example it is interesting to note that although the top rate of commission is 20% and consequently well worth striving for, the actual rate of total commission is only just over 7%

other hand, in looking at the restaurant manager's scheme, it can be seen that because his commission is related to net profit, he has an interest in successfully controlling all aspects of the business, including turnover, purchases, wages, variables, and of course customer satisfaction. In designing an incentive scheme, therefore, one has to ensure that the benefits to the individual do not stimulate him to take measures that may not be in the employer's own interests.

Financial incentives can reward individual employees or groups of employees through increased payment for their increased contribution to the enterprise. However, they can achieve little on their own. They must be part of a comprehensive, well-balanced personnel policy that is based upon offering every employee adequate wages and other conditions before incentives are offered.

FURTHER READING

Currie, Russel M., *Financial Incentives*, Management Publications Ltd., London, 1963.

12 Fringe benefits

The last few years have seen quite important developments in the value and type of fringe benefits that are offered by many organisations to their employees. Some of the major employers in the hotel and catering industry have not been slow to join this trend and nowadays the total number of fringe benefits available to a number of the industry's employees is considerable. There are still many employers, however, who could look into this area of employee compensation, which when properly considered can improve considerably the employees' standard of living – sometimes at little or no cost to the employer.

The importance of fringe benefits in employment policies has grown partly because of high levels of personal tax and partly because of pressure from other sources such as the rapidly increasing competition for employees. Fringe benefits are intended primarily to motivate employees to give better performance and to encourage them to stay with the employer. They include benefits that attract little or no tax such as meals, holidays, cars, and deferred earnings such as pensions. The total list of benefits offered today is considerable and is continually growing as employers look for new ways to woo employees. They can be divided into three main types: financial, part-financial and non-financial.

Financial benefits include : commissions, bonuses, profit sharing, share options.

Part-financial benefits include : pensions, meals, cars, subscriptions.

Non-financial benefits include : holidays, sick pay, medical insurances.

In considering fringe benefits it is vital to recognise that what may be considered an 'incentive' or 'motivator' today may lose its motivating effect with time. This may be because what is offered by only one or two employers to start with will be offered by many employers as they follow suit. Alternatively, what may have been offered as a reward for exceptional service one year becomes expected and a 'matter of right' within the next two or three years.

Having made this point, it is necessary to bear in mind also that although the presence of many fringe benefits in a 'compensation package' may not be a positive incentive to work harder or to perform better, the absence of fringe benefits on the other hand may be a disincentive and will leave an employer at a disadvantage in recruiting or retaining staff.

In some cases offering high salaries, commissions or bonuses may compensate for lack of fringe benefits, but owing to the fact that non-cash benefits are taxed lightly or not at all, these have been playing a bigger part in employee compensation in recent years. They can add another twenty-five per cent to the total payroll costs but a similar increase to salaries, due to high personal tax, would almost certainly not enable employees to purchase the same type of benefits, or to enjoy the same standard of living.

Fringe benefit programmes should be designed to further the employer's objectives and should, in particular, be designed to assist in manpower planning. Where, for example, it is desirable to have a stable, mature management team providing plenty of continuity, such as is required by many brewery companies, a very generous pension and life assurance scheme, along with loan facilities (for house purchasing among other things), will assist in retaining the management team. On the other hand a dynamic young organisation will expect and will want a fairly steady flow of 'whizz kids', the majority of whom will not want to stay for long because there will not be room for all of them. In this case high salaries and good incentive payments will be preferable, as this type of person will not be very interested in pensions – particularly as it is likely that a state scheme will be providing an earnings related scheme some time in the future.

The differing needs of employers along with pressures exerted by competing organisations, and by statutory requirements, will all help to dictate what type of fringe benefits programme needs to be offered. There are many different components and the permutations can be numerous. The major components however are as follows.

FINANCIAL BENEFITS

a) *Commissions and bonuses* These were covered in more detail in Chapter 11 but, as was said there, they should be directly related, as far as possible, to performance. Discretionary 'handouts' have little positive motivational value.

b) *Profit sharing* Although many profit sharing schemes may not be justified directly on motivational grounds, because individuals do not receive a commission or bonus related to their own efforts, and because these awards may be expected as a matter of right, profit sharing may well be justified for indirect reasons. There is a growing view that employees have a proprietorial interest in the undertaking which employs them and that consequently, they should have a share of any increased profits. Awarding a bonus of this kind may not assist directly in increasing profits but withholding an award may have an adverse effect on employees' morale. Whether this share of increased profits should be in the form of a bonus or salary increase depends on current performance of the employer's business. For example, if there is a strong upward trend in profits an increase in salaries could be awarded, whereas if a year's performance was exceptional and not certain to be maintained, a bonus may be preferable from the employer's point of view, because it is a 'once only' payment and because it does not have a gearing up effect on future wage increases, pensions, etc.

c) *Share option schemes* These enable executives to buy options on company shares with loans provided by the employer. The better the company performs the more the value of the executives' shares increases. These schemes are strictly controlled by law; for example, they do not allow an executive to sell his shares until a certain number of years has elapsed.

PART-FINANCIAL BENEFITS

There are many benefits which may be awarded that can be described as partly financial. These are benefits that the employee cannot normally dispose of in cash or kind, but which enable him either to save spending his own resources on these benefits or to enjoy a higher standard of living. These benefits include such things as pensions and life assurance schemes, company cars, expense accounts. The major 'part financial' benefits are as follows.

a) *Pensions* Most schemes grant a fraction of final earnings for each year of service. The better schemes grant 1/60 of final salary (sometimes the average of the last few years) for each year's service, thereby enabling a man with forty or more years' service to retire on forty sixtieths (or two-thirds of final salary) the maximum pension currently permissible. Provision is also normally made for a man's widow whether he dies in service or in retirement.

With the indefinite postponement of the state earnings related pension scheme, which would have provided an earnings related pension, some employers may be tempted to introduce and operate their own schemes.

One of the benefits to employers of comprehensive pension schemes is that they enable employers to retire their older employees, particularly for health reasons, replacing them by younger men, knowing that the older men will be well provided for in retirement.

Currently there are two main types of scheme, the contributory schemes in which the employee has a proprietary right, at least over his own contributions. Upon leaving an employer he can either have his contributions frozen and take a pension upon retirement, or he may transfer his contributions to his new employer's fund. Contributions cost up to about eleven per cent of pay – divided between employer (six per cent) and employee (five per cent).

The other type is the non-contributory scheme in which only the employer pays a contribution and in which employees may not acquire any vested rights. A pension will be paid only if the employee completes his service or at least a certain number of years' service (usually a minimum of ten). The cost of these schemes (around six to seven per cent of pay) is usually less than contributory schemes because those people who leave do not qualify for a pension; however, the contributions paid on their behalf stay in the fund helping to finance the pension of those who do qualify. After April 1975 a person's rights will have to be preserved or transferable.

b) *Life Insurance* In itself this is hardly a benefit that will persuade a man to join one employer rather than another. From the employer's point of view, however, the major value is that it provides for the dependants of employees who die in service. Without this provision the employer may feel that he has a moral, if not a legal responsibility to look after a man's dependants, particularly if the man dies in the course of work. If no insurance is provided some other provision may have to be made on a discretionary basis and, where large numbers of people are employed, cases may be treated inconsistently. In addition the burden may fall more heavily in one year rather than another and, worst of all, if the employer went out of business the dependants of ex-employees may be completely unprovided for.

c) *Company Cars* Generally speaking these are provided for one of two reasons. Firstly it is because an employee needs a car in order to do his job. This would include a variety of people such as regional or area managers and stock takers. Secondly cars are provided to improve a man's standard of living without his incurring the full tax liability that paying an equivalent cash amount would impose.

The provision of company cars is a highly contentious benefit, however, for reasons such as :

1. Cars are very nearly 'cash equivalent' and therefore if a car is provided to one employee in a particular job grade because he needs one, another employee of similar job grade but who does not need or receive a car may well expect the cash equivalent. To complicate this further, if a cash equivalent were paid this would be taxed fully, whereas only part of the estimated value of the car to the other employee would rank for tax.

2. Cars are status symbols both within the organisation and within the community at large and wherever status is concerned people are very sensitive and often irrational.

d) *House purchasing* Purchasing a house is usually the biggest investment that a man ever makes and often moving house is one of the biggest obstacles to employee mobility. (The facts that labour mobility in the hotel and catering industry is high while home ownership by the industry's employees is low are probably not unrelated.) By helping employees to buy a house employers can increase the stability of their labour force. At the top of the scale this assistance can take the form of cheap loans, but, more practically, it can be confined to the employer acting as guarantor for any amount a building society may feel is appropriate.

e) *Removal or relocation expenses* These payments are intended to indemnify an employee for the costs incurred in moving home when being appointed, transferred or promoted by the employer. The amount allowed should be such that the employee is no worse off, nor better off, financially as a direct result of moving house. The expenses included in this however can be extensive, including estate agents costs, legal fees, furniture removal, cost of altering curtains and carpets, new school uniforms, temporary accommodation.

The employer's responsibility must be confined purely to indemnifying the employee for the actual costs incurred in the employee's transfer from one home to another. Considerations of capital appreciation should be excluded.

These are the major part-financial fringe benefits offered by many employers. There are many other others as well which enable employees to enjoy a better standard of living and these include advantageous purchasing of food, liquor, insurances, furniture, etc. These can all be arranged through the employer's own suppliers or agents.

NON-FINANCIAL BENEFITS

Although the main benefits in this category can cost the employer considerable sums of money, they do not normally provide employees with any direct financial advantages. Instead they afford employees other benefits such as a degree of security or more time for leisure.

Fringe benefits are often provided where it is recognised that financial incentives may have little effect due to heavy taxation. The main benefits in this category are :

a) *Holidays* These can be used as a stimulus to labour stability. For example extra days over the minimum can be granted after a certain number of year's service. Extra holiday must be reasonably obtainable however because working for fifteen years for example for extra holiday entitlement will contribute nothing to retaining staff. It is much better to grant two to four extra days after two to four years' service, leading up to an extra week after five years. The table in figure 39 illustrates one example.

Fig.39 Example of a service related holiday entitlement scheme

Years of service	Holiday entitlement per annum
in 1st and 2nd year	3 weeks
in 3rd and 4th year	3 weeks and 2 days
in 5th and 6th year	3 weeks and 4 days
from 7th year onwards	4 weeks

b) *Sick pay schemes.* As with several other conditions of employment details of payment during sickness have to be entered in the statement of conditions of employment. This is required by the Contracts of Employment Act 1963 and, in the absence of such details, an employer may have to pay a sick employee his full wage or salary until he dismisses the employee giving him full notice of termination.

It is for this reason as well as for normal human considerations that employers should formulate a sick pay policy that is consistent with their man management practices and is one that they can afford.

A reasonable arrangement after a qualifying period of service, of say six months to one year, is one month on full pay less state benefits followed by one to two months on two-thirds pay, or in some cases a lesser amount in order to ensure that at no time can an employee actually receive more income whilst sick than he receives whilst working. Medical certificates should of course be presented for any absence through sickness lasting for more than three days.

c) *Private medical treatment.* Private medical treatment is one particular fringe benefit that is being granted to many more employees these days. The direct advantage to the company is that employees can be treated at a time convenient to the company and not when it is convenient to the National Health Service. This is particularly appropriate to key members of the staff. Sometimes the cover provided by the company includes the employee's family as well.

Some employers may feel it too expensive or even inappropriate to pay for this service, but even so employers can arrange 'group rates' and monthly deductions of premiums from salaries enabling their employees to benefit from preferential rates at no cost to the employer. A combination of these two methods can be adopted where senior employees are paid for by the company and the remainder of the employees have the option of participating in the group scheme.

This chapter has dealt with the major benefits that can be offered to employees. All employees will not qualify for all these benefits automatically. Some benefits should be incentives to stay with the organisation and to seek promotion; therefore they should be granted only for service and seniority. On the other hand some may be offered to all employees upon joining, for example discounted purchasing facilities.

Fringe benefits play a vital part in an employer's personnel policy as the nature of all the benefits offered influences considerably the type of employees who will be attracted to the employer and who will stay with him. And since the cost of fringe benefits can add another twenty-five per cent to the payroll cost, it is essential that the range of benefits offered and their likely effects are fully considered.

13 Termination of employment

All the measures examined up to this stage have been concerned with attracting, retaining or motivating employees, but it must be recognised that even if an employer adopted most or all of these practices he would still be faced with people leaving. It is a fact of life that some employees will move on for advancement, some will retire, some will die, and some will have to be dismissed. The most that good personnel practice can and should aim to do, is to reduce staff movements to a level that does not unduly effect the running of the enterprise.

This chapter, therefore, is concerned with the termination of employment, because although some employers have first-rate recruitment, training and remuneration policies, the majority have no formal policies whatever regarding terminations. Instead termination is left entirely to the whims of whichever manager is concerned.

However, because of the increasingly severe staff problems and also because the law – through the Industrial Relations Act – can make 'unfair dismissal' costly to the employer, all termination practices need to be formalised. In order to do this effectively it is essential to have a clear picture of the nature of those employees who leave, and in the larger organisations employing hundreds of people it will be necessary to produce regular analyses of labour turnover. Figure 40 illustrates the form that this type of analysis could take.

Fig. 40 Example of a staff turnover report

SECOND QUARTER

Department	Staff Establishment	No. of leavers in quarter	% for quarter	No. for year cumulative	% for year cumulative
Restaurants	40	8	20%	20	50%
Kitchen	24	2	8.3%	4	16.6%
Front office and Hall porters etc	16	4	25%	4	25%
Housekeeping	40	4	10%	10	25%
TOTAL	120	18	15%	28	23%

Figure 40 shows a very simple example and more complex analyses may include such statistical methods as Moving Average Totals (M.A.T.s), and cumulative totals, which can show further breakdowns into such factors as age, marital status, reasons for termination. In the largest undertakings these would be done monthly, and in medium-sized organisations quarterly or half-yearly. They would not be necessary for individually owned or managed undertakings with only a small number of employees.

Analyses of this kind will show periodic increases or decreases in staff turnover by individual departments. It is then the task of management to discover the reasons for such increases which may include :

1. Wage and salary rates falling behind the rates offered by competitors.
2. Better conditions generally (such as reduction in split shifts, or a five-day week) being offered by competitors.
3. The decline in quality of supervision and departmental managers.
4. Recruitment, selection, induction and training practices needing improvement.

Both the staff turnover report itself and the information deduced from such reports are of a statistical nature, that is, they are mainly concerned with groups and numbers of people. The actual termination procedures adopted however are concerned with individuals and these are divided into two main types : voluntary, where the employees leave of their own free will, and involuntary, where the employer decides that employment should terminate.

VOLUNTARY TERMINATION

Almost invariably this arises where an employee has the opportunity to take other employment that offers more attractive conditions, but, because employees leaving voluntarily have not been dismissed by the employer, they are probably the employees that an employer would most like to retain. It is for this reason that these employees should be interviewed to determine their reasons for leaving. The *exit* interview may reveal specific information regarding conditions of employment, competitors' conditions, the quality or otherwise of supervision, training and selection procedures. Finally a well conducted exit interview can assure that employees leave on good terms. Ex-employees are, after all, to some extent an employer's ambassadors, broadcasting his reputation among other potential employees. In some cases it may be advisable to supplement an exit interview by talking to a departing employee's past supervisor in order to check the reasons given by the employee.

INVOLUNTARY TERMINATIONS

In this industry, along with some others, dismissal is often used as the first remedy for a variety of ills, rather than being used as the last. In fact, in some sectors of the industry dismissals are quite indiscriminate. For example, it is common practice for complete bar staffs to be dismissed because of bad liquor stock results. The innocent suffer the same fate (dismissal) as the guilty.

One recognises that pilferage in this industry is a serious problem, but other measures such as more methodical selection, better conditions of employment, and better career prospects, along with stricter and more accurate means of control, are better solutions than indiscriminate sackings. Where pilferers are caught however they should be prosecuted rather than being allowed to get away with their crime, often because the employer wants no trouble or publicity.

The dismissal of an employee is a very serious measure particularly now that the law provides employees with protection against unfair dismissal. The law on dismissals is dealt with in more detail in Chapter 15.

The vast majority of terminations, however, are not a consequence of pilferage, and in most cases are as unwanted by the employer as by the employee. The most common reasons are :

1. Lack of ability
2. Continual late arrival, absenteeism, or disobedience
3. Personality.

In all these cases when contemplating dismissal other remedies should be considered first. For example, lack of ability may well be the fault of the employer because he did not select or place the employee carefully enough, or because he did not provide appropriate training. In the second case tighter discipline could possibly overcome the problem and a discussion with the employee to discover the underlying causes would possibly be helpful. In the third case, if it is a 'clash of personalities', and if the organisation is big enough, a transfer may be the solution. On the other hand, once a decision is made to terminate employment it must always be borne in mind that the employer may have to prove in an industrial tribunal that the dismissal was 'fair', as laid down in the Industrial Relations Act. Documentary evidence, therefore, of unsatisfactory work or behaviour, and of warnings given may prove vital in proving the case. It is important therefore to operate a formal system of warnings that can be used as a last resort by the employer should he be called in front of an industrial tribunal. Typical warnings could look like these shown in figure 41.

Fig.41 Examples of written warnings

1 April 1974

MEMO

To AN Other   From T Boss

Further to my discussion with you this morning I should like to confirm that your constant late arrivals for duty must cease otherwise I shall be forced to consider terminating your employment.

10 April 1974

MEMO

To AN Other   From T Boss

Further to my memorandum of 1 April and to our discussion this morning, I should like to record that if there are any further occurrences of late arrival, without legitimate reason, your services with the company will no longer be required.

REDUNDANCY

The other main form of involuntary termination is of course
redundancy. This is where a man's job is eliminated owing to such
things as changes in methods, rationalisation, or mergers. In this
case the law lays down certain minimal payments to be made to
the employee. These are shown in figure 45 (see Chapter 15). The
employer , who has to contribute to the redundancy fund, recovers
fifty per cent of the cost from the fund. In addition to this payment
some employers, recognising the inadequacy of the amounts
awarded by the Redundancy Payment Act, allow what is known
sometimes as 'severance pay'. This is additional to redundancy
pay and is usually calculated by using some formula that recognises
age, service and present earnings. Employers must recognise, however, that redundancies are sometimes the fault of their own lack
of forward planning. If planning, and this includes manpower
planning, is conducted thoroughly, many redundancies can be
avoided by allowing natural wastage to reduce the labour force.
But once it becomes apparent that redundancies are unavoidable
this fact should be discussed with employee representatives so that
plans for a properly phased run-down can be agreed. This may
include voluntary early retirements and compensation payments
for voluntary terminations. In some cases it may be essential to
keep employees working to a certain date in which case special
'incentive payments' to stay in the job will have to be agreed.

RETIREMENT

The last type of termination is of course when a man goes into
retirement and these days some of the more enlightened employers
recognise that their responsibility extends beyond providing a
pension and a gold watch. In fact they provide some form of pre-
retirement preparation that enables a man to adjust to his
completely changed circumstances, because not only does he
suddenly have greatly increased free time, but his income may
drop considerably and his contact with friends and colleagues may
be reduced.

EXIT INTERVIEWS

The importance of interviewing employees when they leave was
touched upon briefly earlier in this chapter, but it cannot be over-
emphasised that the numbers and types of people leaving an

organisation are critical indications of the success or otherwise of an employer's personnel and employee relations policy. Employees leaving can be a valuable source from which to learn where improvements in personnel practice can be made. With few exceptions therefore all employees should be interviewed before their departure, in order to :

1. Learn the real reasons for their departure (unless these are patently obvious).
2. Pin-point trouble spots and causes of irritation and frustration.
3. Inform employees of all their benefits and rights, such as pensions, and insurances. In the case of pensioners they will need to know what rights they retain such as insurances, holidays and discount purchasing facilities.
4. Explain the make-up of the final pay cheque including such items as holiday pay.
5. Hand over the P45 and insurance cards or obtain a forwarding address.
6. Collect any company property that may be outstanding such as cash advances, equipment, uniforms, protective clothing.
7. Part on friendly terms, if possible, so that ex-employees act as 'ambassadors'.

WHO DISMISSES?

The question of who actually dismisses employees is a contentious one. Many line managers feel that they need to have this right as a support to, and indication of, their authority. Others, on the other hand, would dearly like to abdicate the responsibility to someone else such as a personnel officer. However because line managers, in the last resort, are responsible for the results of their departments they must carry this burden and they must make the decision assisted and guided by specialists, where they are employed, such as personnel officers. In many circumstances it is best for the 'grandfather' principle to be applied to dismissals. This means that no man can dismiss his immediate subordinates without the approval of his own superior. Furthermore in large organisations the approval of the personnel officer or department should also be obtained because they will know if any opportunities exist for an employee about to be dismissed.

The turnover of staff is the barometer of the success or otherwise of an employer's personnel management policies. Generally speaking the higher the rate of turnover the poorer are his relationships with his employees and the lower the turnover the better the relationships. High labour turnover often results in low levels of efficiency. It incurs high costs in recruitment and training and results in customer dissatisfaction. In most cases, therefore, when an employee leaves an employer, the employer should examine the circumstances very carefully to see whether he is in some way responsible for what is, after all, some degree of failure on his part. He may have failed the employee for a variety of reasons including wrong selection or placement in the first place, inadequate training, unsatisfactory conditions of employment or just poor management.

14 Industrial relations

The term industrial relations is generally used to describe the relationship that exists between the management of an undertaking and its work people, usually organised and represented within a trade union framework. In the hotel and catering industry the degree of organisation of employees within trade unions varies considerably. At one end of the scale, industrial and institutional catering, more than sixty per cent of all employees' conditions of employment are determined by collective bargaining; yet at the other end of the scale, hotels and restaurants, the number of trade union members is negligible.

The attitude of management in the industry towards trade unions varies considerably too. Generally speaking, those managers with experience of trade unions accept their existence and believe that they have a useful role to play. On the other hand most vociferous opponents of trade unions are to be found among those hotel and restaurant proprietors and managers who by and large have no experience of trade unions and who may never have spoken to union officials or shop stewards in their lives.

In spite of such resistance, together with the apathy of many employees, the recommendations contained in the Commission on Industrial Relations (CIR) reports, the work of the industry's little Neddy, the Industrial Relations Act, and the trade unions themselves, are almost certain to increase the role of trade unions in the industry in the long term, even though currently the industry's labour force is not organised within the trade union movement to the same extent as many other workers. There are a variety of reasons for this including :

1. The large numbers of small establishments that make it difficult for trade union officials to contact potential members and to organise meetings.

2. The highly dispersed and departmentalised labour force, even in the largest establishments, resulting in the absence of cohesive groups of workers with common interests.

3. The large number of female and part-time employees who are not interested in belonging to a trade union.

4. The large number of foreign employees who are in the United Kingdom for short periods of time.

5. Shift working, which makes it difficult to contact and organise employees.

6. Tipping, which introduces an 'entrepreneurial' element into work, which many employees fear a trade union would try to eliminate.

7. No tradition of trade union membership within the industry.

8. Employers' resistance, because employers fear that they have more to lose than to gain from the trade union movement.

These are probably the major reasons for the low level of trade union activity within the industry. However, in order to see the hotel and catering industry's industrial relations in perspective it is important to look at industrial relations generally and in particular to examine the development of organisations of work people and of employers.

DEVELOPMENT OF THE TRADE UNION MOVEMENT

The organisation of employers and workers came about from the eighteenth century onwards with the emergence of modern industry. Before this time most conditions of employment had been regulated by the State, often through the local magistrate, and it was an offence in common law to do anything (even with the intention of improving one's own conditions of work) which might have been in restraint of trade. A combination of workers, therefore, to strike or to do anything else to improve conditions that adversely affected the employer's business, was a criminal act of conspiracy. But at the same time it was illegal for employers to form such combinations. As industry became more complex the State regulation of wages fell into disuse and employers themselves were able to fix the conditions of employment. Legislation followed banning combinations in one trade after another until the situation was made quite clear when the Combination Acts 1799–1800 provided for a general prohibition in all trades of combinations of employees or employers.

However, following the Napoleonic Wars there was an economic depression together with a movement to improve conditions which resulted in the repeal, in 1824, of the Combination Laws. The effect of this was to allow workers to enter into combinations for the purpose of regulating wages and other conditions without their committing the crime of conspiracy. This Act (the Combination Laws Repeal Act 1824) was followed shortly by another which somewhat circumscribed workers' rights but it still preserved the right to withhold labour by collective action and this right has never been withdrawn.

Subsequent acts, including the Trade Union Act 1871 and the Conspiracy and Protection of Property Act 1875, gave trade unions legal status and also permitted peaceful picketing. Then the Trade Disputes Act 1906 protected a trade union from being sued for alleged wrongful acts committed by it or on its behalf. Thus trade unions were freed of any risk of a *civil* liability arising from their actions. A variety of other legislation followed which repealed certain preceding legislation, covered the amalgamation of trade unions, and tidied up some other aspects that were not satisfactory.

However, the most notable legislation to date is the Industrial Relations Act of 1971, which replaced most preceding legislation regarding trade unions and followed both the main political parties' examination of the increasingly complex and potentially disruptive industrial relations scene. This Act granted to an individual for the first time the right to belong or not to belong to a Trade Union. It created a new legal concept of 'unfair industrial practice'. It also granted the government the right (in grave circumstances) to order a trade union to refrain from taking certain industrial action, such as striking or working to rule, for a limited period of up to a maximum of sixty days. In addition it laid down a code for good industrial relations practice.

PRESENT POSITION

The Trade Union Movement, along with other sectors of our society, is going through a period of mergers and rationalisations, and although at the end of 1972 there were about 480 trade unions whose members totalled about eleven million, seventy-five per cent of those members were members of only twenty-three unions.

In some cases there is strong competition among unions for membership, and one notable case was in fact in this industry where the Transport and General Workers' Union and the National Union of General and Municipal Workers came into conflict over recruiting hotel workers in Torquay.

The strength of the trade union movement obviously comes from its ability to present a united front, and therefore many individual unions join federations to further strengthen their movement. At the end of 1972 the number of federations was forty-seven. These federations are however, in most cases rather loose, and the responsibility for action rests with the individual unions.

The whole trade union movement, with a few exceptions such as the National Association of Licensed House Managers in the case of the hotel and catering industry, comes together within the Trades Union Congress (TUC), the aims of which are:

'To promote the interests of all its affiliated organisations and generally to improve the economic and social conditions of workers.'

The TUC, as with the federations of unions, has little authority over individual unions, but it does oblige affiliated unions to keep its General Council informed of any trade disputes that may involve large numbers of work people.

THE ROLE OF TRADE UNIONS

Trade unions are primarily concerned with representing their members in order to obtain what is considered by their members to be a fair share of the revenue generated by their employers.

Although unions are concerned with obtaining increased earnings they also strive to improve their members' other conditions of employment such as time off, holidays, safety and status. They have in addition shown particular concern over job security.

EMPLOYERS' ASSOCIATIONS

The first employers' associations were probably the merchant guilds and livery companies which existed throughout Europe from the early Middle Ages. They dealt with a variety of matters that affected trade and labour.

With the repeal of the combination laws and because of pressure from the growing trade union movement employers' organisations grew rapidly during the nineteenth century. Nowadays they are, generally speaking, organised on a trade or industry-wide basis and because of this they deal with matters of trade, such as encouraging government to take defensive measures against foreign competition, and with matters of employment, such as negotiating industry-wide conditions of employment.

These employers' or trade associations come together in various national bodies, the main being the Confederation of British Industries, which has individual employers, trade associations, employers' organisations, and nationalised industries within its membership. The British Hotels, Restaurants and Caterers' Association, and the Brewers' Society are the hotel and catering industry's principal trade or employers' associations.

The conduct of negotiation and consultation varies considerably from employer to employer and from industry to industry. In some cases all negotiations will take place at national level between the trade union concerned and the employers' association. This is sometimes referred to as the 'formal' system. In other cases all discussions and negotiations will take place 'informally' at plant level, that is, between the local employer and his own employees.

INDUSTRIAL RELATIONS IN THE HOTEL AND CATERING INDUSTRY

Trade union membership within the hotel and catering industry is, generally speaking, very low. Estimates are that, excluding industrial and institutional catering, there are about 40,000 members (including the 10,000 members of the National Association of Licensed House Managers). This means that probably less than five per cent of the total labour force are union members. Membership is relatively strong in the industrial and institutional catering sector (about twenty per cent of all employees) because the catering staff are frequently part of a large totally unionised work force (such as in the motor industry). There are a few other isolated exceptions including British Transport Hotels and also some hotels and towns where union membership is relatively strong. Figure 42 shows the degree of trade union involvement in the industry.

Fig.42 The principle unions involved in the hotel, catering and associated industries

Section of the hotel and catering industry	Approx. No. of employees*	Principle unions involved		Approx. % of union members
1. Hotels and restaurants	230,000	GMWU	The General and Municipal Workers Union	20,000
		TGWU	The Transport and General Workers Union	3,000
		NUR	The National Union of Railwaymen	3,000
		TSSA	The Transport Salaried Staff Association	
		USDAW	The Union of Shop, Distributive and Allied Workers	1,000
				2,600
2. Industrial and institutional	220,000	GMWU		30,000
		TGWU		8,000
		USDAW		
3. Public house managers	14,500	NALHM	The National Association of Licensed House Managers	10,000
		ACTSS	The Association of Clerical, Technical, and Supervisory Staff (Section of TGWU)	500
4. Club stewards	16,500	UFUCS	The United Federation and Union of Club Stewards and Hotel Managers of Great Britain	1,300
		GCSA	The Golf Club Stewards' Association	350
5. Bar staff	200,000	GMWU		less than 5,000
		TGWU		
		USDAW		

* The numbers quoted refer to those persons within scope of the appropriate wages council

WAGES COUNCILS

In 1945 with the enactment of the Wages Councils Act and the creation of wages boards it was recognised that where employees were not organised there was insufficient pressure on employers to ensure that wage levels and other conditions kept up with those offered to other sections of the community. In this industry this had been recognised earlier and resulted in the Catering Wages Act of 1943 which created the Catering Wages Board. This board laid down minimum conditions of employment. However this Act and others have since been superseded by the Wages Council Act 1959 which regulates wages and other conditions for employees in the industry through wages councils which include employer and employee representatives. Councils exist for the following sectors of the industry :

Licensed residential establishments and restaurants
Licensed non-residential establishments and restaurants
Unlicensed places of refreshment.

The rates laid down by the various councils, however, are considered by most employers and employees to be absolute minima and market forces generally oblige employers to pay well above these rates. The value of wages councils nowadays is therefore questionable and it is hoped by many that these will be phased out. In fact the CIR report on Industrial Catering (in 1973) recommended the abolition of the Wages Council for Industrial and Staff Canteens.

RESPONSIBILITY FOR GOOD INDUSTRIAL RELATIONS

The responsibility for good industrial relations depends, within each undertaking, upon its management, and this can only result from frank discussion between management and staff. The Industrial Relations Code of Practice places the responsibility for stimulating this dialogue squarely on management. In the section on communication and consultation (paragraph 59 of the code) it says :

'Management in co-operation with employee representatives should :

   i)   provide opportunities for employees to discuss matters affect-
       ing their jobs with those to whom they are responsible;
  ii)   ensure that managers are kept informed of the views of
       employees and of the problems which they may face in
       meeting management's objectives.'

This responsibility is quite clearly laid down but in this industry
the CIR report on Hotels and Restaurants found that a major
problem for staff was 'little opportunity to put their views to
management on matters which concerned them'.

If good industrial relations are to be achieved discussion must
take place between management and staff on all matters related
to conditions and methods of work. The size of the organisation
does not affect this principle; the only variation to it is one of
degree, as the actual size and nature of the organisation determines
the type and degree of formality of discussions.

Within this industry there are probably three main types of
consultative or negotiating procedure. The first and probably the
least formal will be found in the individually owned hotel or
restaurant, managed by the proprietor who works in the establishment with his staff numbering up to about twenty. In this case
any formal joint consultation or negotiation should be unnecessary
as the employer is close to his employees and should be aware of
their problems and views. It is his job to keep himself informed of
their opinions and feelings and he may well hold informal meetings
at regular intervals with all staff. Such meetings may already be
held to discuss menus, special functions etc., and from time to time
they should be enlarged to cover methods of work and conditions
of employment.

The next level may be found in a hotel or restaurant probably
having groups of employees in several departments. Typically this
would be a hotel or restaurant complex with from twenty to several
hundred employees. In this case there may be small groups of
people working together – each group with its own aims – often
not the same as those of the organisation as a whole. One only
needs to think of the conflict between cooks and waiters in many
hotels or restaurants to accept that this conflict exists. In this case
each department should nominate a representative to meet management's representatives on a regular basis – probably between four
and eight times a year. Some formality would be needed and
agendas would have to be circulated beforehand and minutes
produced afterwards.

The level after this would be in a company or organisation with several large units. Each establishment would have its own joint consultative committee, and in addition it may find it worth organising a company based joint consultative committee with representatives from each establishment meeting head office management. This system would be most appropriate where a company is heavily represented in an area – London for example – and because management would wish to discourage unnecessary movement between units caused by varying supervisory or personnel practices within the company's establishments. On the other hand it may not be necessary where an employer's establishments are located far apart in areas where conditions are different.

These are the three main degrees or levels of consultation (and possibly negotiation), but whether all three should be conducted with trade union representatives or not is generally for management and the employees to decide. It is probably unnecessary, and even inappropriate, in many cases for the smaller establishment but the second and third levels, involving the larger employers, certainly could involve trade union representatives. Whether employers will wish to enter into agency shop agreements (a type of closed shop) also will depend on the particular circumstances, but employers must remember that a ballot by employees can make such an agreement compulsory for an employer.

BENEFITS OF CONSULTATION

Managers must rightly ask what benefits can result from their taking the initiative in establishing joint consultation and even bargaining or negotiating procedures with their employees. Firstly and most important of all, it must be recognised that although employees may have no negotiating machinery they still push up rates of pay and win other concessions by 'voting with their feet'. They move from employer to employer continually looking for higher earnings and employers in turn have continually to increase their rates to attract replacement staff. Seasonal resorts will confirm that this practice is rife. The fear of 'run-away' wage increases consequently is generally exaggerated. Instead, because of continuous collective pressure from the employees their conditions would steadily improve, job security would become greater with the result that the staff turnover rate would almost certainly drop to reasonable proportions. There are many cases in those sections of the industry where trade unions are strong, where the annual staff turnover is not above ten per cent per annum. As a result the economies to be made through not having to recruit and train a steady flow of replacement staff are considerable, apart from the benefits of being able to maintain consistent standards.

A second benefit of consultation is a more willing acceptance of change. By nature must people oppose change, but if they have been involved in discussing changes that affect them and they understand the underlying reasons, they will almost certainly be more prepared to make the changes work. A further benefit is that many work people have ideas that can improve working methods, and by consultation management can provide the opportunities for these to be expressed.

DISADVANTAGES

On the other side of the coin there are disadvantages to be faced when entering into consultation with employees. Firstly management action will be open to question and discussion, with the consequence that management's decisions and practices will have to be so much better. Furthermore even confidential information must be made available for discussion. Apart from this it must be remembered that if trade unions are involved the possibility of industrial action such as working to rule, blacking, banning overtime and even striking must not be ruled out when agreement on such things as pay, working conditions, methods or procedures cannot be reached.

THE INDUSTRY'S IMAGE

Of less immediate consequence to the individual employer, but of great importance to the industry as a whole, is the need to improve its image. The supply of continental staff is running down owing to increased standards of living in the traditional suppliers of catering staff and also because of our own government's action to reduce unemployment at home. The industry, therefore, has to attract an ever growing share of the domestic work force.

To improve its image the hotel and catering industry needs to offer conditions that satisfy the average working man's expectations, and this will only be achieved through regular, frank consultation and negotiation between both sides, as happens in many other industries. Without this dialogue and the consequent improvement in conditions the industry will not attract the number of competent work people that are going to be needed in the future.

ESTABLISHING CONSULTATION

Once the decision has been taken to establish consultation within an organisation, the scope of any discussions must not be limited, but should cover *all matters* of interest to both sides, including rates of pay, hours of work, fringe benefits, working methods, and company plans. (The IR Act made the disclosure of certain information statutory in organisations with over 350 employees.)

Fig.43 Example of constitution and rules for a joint consultative committee

Aim

The purpose of the Joint Consultative Committee is to establish and maintain an effective system of communication between the company's management and its employees so that by consultation the well-being of both sides may be promoted.

Constitution

1.   The Committee shall consist of one staff representative from each department

2.   Management shall be represented by the general manager, the assistant manager (personnel) and one other member of line management

3.   The chairman will be a member of management

4.   The secretary will be nominated by management

Rules

1.   Meetings shall take place not less than once every six weeks. Either side may call a meeting as necessary by notifying the secretary. In this case the meeting must take place within three weeks

2.   The quorum shall be one management representative and more than half of the elected staff representatives or their substitutes

3.   Elected representatives unable to attend a meeting may nominate a substitute, who must come from the representative's department

4.   Subjects of mutual interest regarding methods of work and conditions of employment may be discussed by the JCC with the exception that no individual employee's case may be discussed

5.   Rules may be altered or otherwise amended by mutual agreement

Setting up a joint consultative committee sometimes presents problems, because it is essential that the employees' representatives are chosen, and seen to be chosen by their colleagues and not by management. The following steps may be taken to achieve this.

1. Employees, known to be respected by their colleagues, should be called from each department to attend a meeting with representatives of management. At this meeting the intention of establishing a joint consultative committee should be explained by a senior member of management.

2. If the idea is accepted the representatives should be asked to discuss this with their departmental colleagues, and if the reaction of the majority of employees appears to be in favour of the consultative committee a ballot should then be organised in each department to elect the departmental representative. The elected representatives should then be given the opportunity to hold a meeting at which they would elect their own officers.

3. A further meeting would then be held between the *elected* representatives and the representatives of management where procedures would be agreed for the future.

The outline of a constitution and rules for a joint consultative committee is illustrated in figure 43.

FURTHER READING

Anthony, Peter and Crichton, Anne, *Industrial Relations and the Personnel Specialists,* Batsford, London, 1969.

CIR Report 27; *The Hotel and Catering Industry*
      Part I   Hotels and Restaurants
      Part II   Industrial Catering
      Part III   Public houses, clubs and other sectors
                                  H.M.S.O., London, 1972.

Industrial Relations, Industrial Society, London, 1972.

15 Law of employment

The evolution and development of our complex industrial society has been accompanied by the need to regulate many of the activities of various groups of people. In particular the activities of employers needed to be regulated by law to ensure that employees were provided with adequate physical and social safeguards. This need for legal regulation has come about partly because competitive pressures do not permit individual employers to invest in non-productive areas (however much they may like to) without jeopardising their own competitive position. When, on the other hand, all employers are compelled by law to make similar investments in improving working conditions few of them suffer unduly in relation to their competitors.

Until fairly recent times in our history, responsibility for regulating conditions of employment rested largely on parliament and on local magistrates. This was relatively easy whilst the number of categories of workers was small. Gradually, however, as society became more industrialised it became increasingly difficult to exercise this control. The pendulum swung the other way. As was seen in the last chapter various laws were passed that made it possible for both workers and owners to combine into trade unions and associations in order to bargain, until the stage was reached where the State appeared to avoid any direct involvement in the relationships between employers and employees. The whole system of bargaining and negotiation then rested on voluntary understandings between the workers and their employers. However, as our industrial society developed even further the power of trade unions grew and the concentration of certain vital resources and services into what became vulnerable positions made it possible for many groups of people to disrupt supplies to the whole community.

The government therefore felt obliged to re-enter the field of relations between employers and employees by creating a legal framework for the conduct of what is now called industrial relations.

The government's responsibility rests with a senior cabinet minister, the Secretary of State for Employment. In addition, several other ministers have responsibilities that are related to employment and these include the Secretary of State for Social Services who is concerned with such matters as national insurance and pensions, and the Secretary for Trade and Industry who is responsible for such matters as regional development policy.

The law relating to employment is considerable now and it is only possible in this book to cover a small part of it. The major areas of legislation have been selected and are summarised below.

CONTRACTS OF EMPLOYMENT

A contract of employment is the basis of the working relationship between employer and employee and is subject to the general principles covered by the law of contract. Consequently a contract of employment may be verbal, written, or the terms may be merely implied. It consists of an offer by one of the parties and an acceptance by the other. A *consideration,* that is, an exchange of promises to perform certain duties and to pay certain wages and provide certain conditions, is necessary to create the contract. The *consideration,* as with all contracts, must have an economic value. The offer is usually (but not necessarily) made by the employer and should contain details of remuneration, hours, location and holidays. The offer may refer to other documents such as wages council publications. Not all conditions have to be included as some may be implied by custom and practice. The contract comes into existence when the offerer receives acceptance from the offeree.

Although contracts need not be in writing it is recommended strongly that all offers and their acceptance be properly documented, to avoid misunderstanding and to minimise the likelihood of litigation.

Nowadays most terms within a contract existing between employer and employee are covered by the Contracts of Employment Act 1972.

CONTRACTS OF EMPLOYMENT ACT 1972

This Act establishes the rights of employees, who work over a certain number of hours, to minimum periods of notice dependent on their length of service, and the Act also requires that employees are given written details of certain conditions of employment.

The minimum lengths of notice after thirteen weeks have been completed are shown in figure 44.

Fig.44 Contracts of Employment Act, 1972, minimum periods of notice

Length of continuous service	Minimum notice
Less than 13 weeks	Not specified*
13 weeks but less than 2 years	1 week
2 years but less than 5 years	2 weeks
5 years but less than 10 years	4 weeks
10 years but less than 15 years	6 weeks
15 years or more	8 weeks

The employer has the right to receive one week's notice of termination from all employees who have completed 13 weeks employment. This period does not lengthen with longer service.

* Although the period of notice is not specified by the Act in this case the pay period (e.g. one week) should be taken as the minimum period unless a specified trial or probationary period has been agreed between the two parties.

Where a contract provides for longer periods of notice the terms of the contract will apply, whereas contracts containing shorter periods are overridden by the periods laid down by the Contracts of Employment Act. Payment in lieu of notice may be made by the employer or the employee.

Written particulars All employees who work for more than twenty-one hours each week and who have been employed for thirteen weeks or more are to be given written particulars of their Conditions of Employment, and these must include :

1. Employer's name
2. Employee's name
3. Commencing date
4. Rate of pay, including overtime rates and the method of calculation
5. Frequency and method of payment
6. Hours of duty and compulsory overtime
7. Holiday entitlement and rights to accrued holiday pay
8. Sick pay arrangements (if none exists this must be stated)
9. Pension scheme arrangements (if none exists this must be stated)
10. Notice of termination
11. Rights regarding trade union membership and recognition of specific trade unions
12. Procedure for registering complaints or grievances
13. The date at which these conditions applied which must not be more than a week before the statement is given to the employee.

The statement must also say that any changes to conditions will be notified in writing within one month of the change taking place. Such changes must have the agreement of the employee concerned although where he does not agree to the revised terms it is quite possible, subject to the 'unfair dismissal' provisions, to give him notice and to offer re-engagement on the revised terms.

Written statements need not take any particular form and they can refer employees to other documents such as manuals and booklets which must be reasonably available to them. There is no requirement in law for the employee or the employer to sign the statement. But it is very advisable to issue all employees with a statement and to retain signed copies in the personal dossiers. The ideal way administratively is to design letters of offer so that they satisfy the Contracts of Employment Act requirements. An example is shown in figure 21 (Chapter 5).

RESTRAINT ON EMPLOYEES

In the case of some employees, such as chefs or managers, employers feel it necessary to include a clause in a contract restraining an employee from divulging trade secrets, entering into direct competition by operating his own business, working for another person in the same line of business or using lists of customers prepared in the course of employment in order to entice customers away.

In order to obtain protection against such eventualities any terms in a contract need to be clearly stated and not implied. It is important however to make such a term reasonable in the circumstances otherwise the right to any protection could be forfeited. At the same time such restraint clauses must be shown to be in the public interest. For example it may be that a clause restraining a chef from working in a particular area would not be upheld if there was a severe shortage of chefs.

SEARCHING EMPLOYEES

It is always advisable to obtain an employee's permission before attempting to search him or his property. To search a person without permission, and without finding evidence of theft, can result in the employer being prosecuted for assault and battery. In those cases where the employer's right to search is considered to be vital, such as in hotels and industrial catering organisations, a clause to this effect should be written into every person's contract of employment.

DISMISSALS

Unfair dismissal The Industrial Relations Act 1971 introduced protection for employees against unfair dismissal.

In the past so long as an employer gave the agreed period of notice or money in lieu an employee had no recourse against the employer. The situation has changed now and the employer has to show that reasons for dismissal were fair. Valid reasons include :

1. Lack of capability or qualification for the job for which an employee was employed

2. Misconduct
3. Redundancy, within the definition of the Redundancy Payments Act 1965
4. Unsuitability due to legal restrictions, such as the employment, in certain circumstances, of young persons in the licensed parts of an establishment
5. Some other substantial reason which could justify dismissal.

It should be noted that no complaint of unfair dismissal or of a worker's rights relating to trade unions will be heard by an industrial tribunal until a Department of Employment conciliation officer has looked into the circumstances to see if a settlement can be reached without a tribunal hearing.

Instant or summary dismissal In certain instances an employer may be justified in dismissing an employee without giving the required period of notice nor money in lieu. Although this may be permitted in such cases as an employee's permanent incapacity to perform his duties, in most cases it is used where employees are guilty of serious misconduct. To dismiss a person instantly can have serious consequences for the employer, if a dismissed employee sues him successfully for damages, so it is not a step to be taken lightly. Reasons for instant dismissal include :

1. Serious or repeated disobedience or other misconduct
2. Serious or repeated negligence
3. Drunkenness while on duty
4. Theft
5. Accepting bribes or commissions.

An employer can normally only dismiss an employee for misconduct committed outside working hours and away from the place of work if other employees were involved, which could have an effect on the employer's business, or if the employee is in domestic service.

Where an employer dismisses a person instantly it should be done at the time of the misdemeanour or when it first comes to the attention of the employer. To delay will imply that the employer has waived his right to dismiss. The reason for dismissal should be given at the time of the dismissal.

An employer may in some cases withhold money earned by an employee who has been instantly dismissed for good reasons, unless a contract states otherwise. However legal advice should always be sought before taking such action.

PAYMENT OF WAGES

THE TRUCK ACTS

These Acts referring mainly to manual workers impose restrictions on the 'truck' system whereby employers were able to oblige their workers to spend part or all of their earnings on goods sold to them by the employer. Also the Truck Acts provide that payment of wages may not be made in kind, nor can the price of goods supplied on credit be recovered by deduction from wages. No deductions may be made from workmen's wages unless certain strict regulations are followed or unless they are permitted by statute. Where employers are authorised to provide their work people with fuel, accommodation, tools or medical attendance, deductions may be made from wages, provided each workman's consent is obtained in writing.

PAYMENT OF WAGES ACT 1960

This Act modified the Truck Acts' requirement that wages be paid in cash. Wages can now be paid by cheque, postal or money order or into a bank account by such means as bank credit transfer. Employees can insist on receiving their pay in cash or they can ask that their wages be paid in one of the above forms. An employer may refuse such a request however and can insist on paying in cash. For any form of payment, therefore, other than cash, agreement from both parties is required.

The Act also provides that a 'pay statement' be issued, before or on each occasion a wage payment is made. This statement will include :

    i)   Gross pay
   ii)   Details of each deduction
  iii)   Net pay
  iv)   Where payment is made in other than cash the net amount of each type of payment.

Where deductions are fixed details need not be given on each occasion. However, these details must be given at least once every twelve months and also whenever a fixed deduction changes.

ATTACHMENT OF EARNINGS ACT 1971

This Act enables a court to order an employer to make periodic deductions from an employee's earnings and to pay the sum deducted to the collecting officer of the court. The court specifies the amount and can make *priority orders* for payment of fines or maintenance of dependants, or *non-priority* orders for the clearance of civil debts. The court will also specify the *protected earnings* which is the level of income below which a man's earnings should not be reduced by these deductions. Any consequent shortfalls in payments will be carried forward.

SUSPENSIONS

In some circumstances, particularly involving alleged misconduct, an employer may wish to suspend an employee until the circumstances have been looked into and a decision taken regarding the employee's future. It is quite in order to do this so long as pay is not withheld – unless a contract specifically permitting the withholding of pay is in existence.

P.A.Y.E.

Under the Income and Corporation Taxes Act 1970 employers are obliged to deduct tax payable on money paid to any of their employees earning money falling under Schedule E (that is, emoluments from any office or employment).

The following items are not normally taxable :

1. Business expenses
2. Rent free accommodation or temporary accommodation allowances which are provided because of the nature of the employer's business
3. Money paid in lieu of notice
4. Luncheon vouchers under 15p in value or where they exceed 15p only the excess will be taxable.

EMPLOYER'S LIABILITY

There are two separate categories of liability that employers bear in relation to injuries suffered by their employees whilst in their employment. These are common law and statutory liabilities.

The common law responsibilities extend also to employees of other employers, such as contractors, whilst working on the employer's premises, and also to the employer's employees carrying out work for him on another person's premises, for example, an outdoor caterer's staff.

In common law employers are expected to provide protection that is reasonable in the circumstances. An employee will be compensated for injury if the employer was at fault in exposing the employee to unnecessary risk in the circumstances.

Unfortunately the common law is not able to provide for all developments in industry and therefore several statutes exist to specify the nature of protection to be provided and to lay down certain other regulations covering the working environment.

OFFICE, SHOPS AND RAILWAY PREMISES ACT 1963

This Act was introduced in order to protect the health, safety and welfare of employees in offices, shops and railway premises. The Act covers any building where the sole or principal use is the carrying on of retail trade or business, and this definition included the sale of food or drink for immediate consumption to members of the public.

This is very comprehensive, detailed legislation and its provisions include the following:

a)   Cleanliness.

b)   Overcrowding; for example, each person must have not less than 40 sq. ft of floor space, or where ceilings are below 10 ft in height each person must have not less than 400 cu. ft.

c)   Temperature, ventilation, lighting, eating and sanitary facilities; minimum standards are laid down for each of these.

d)   Training. Staff employed on dangerous machines such as: mincing machines, dough mixers, vegetable slicers, food mixing machines, bacon slicers, potato chippers (whether power-driven or not), must receive appropriate training.

e)   First aid boxes and facilities. The Act requires that first aid boxes are provided in all places of work and that trained first aiders are available in offices and shops where more than fifty persons are employed.

f) Other provisions cover : fire precautions, drinking water supply, locker accommodation, sitting facilities, young persons, floor covering, use of dangerous machinery, notification of accidents, registration of premises.

FACTORIES ACT 1961

This Act generally covers those premises in which persons are employed as manual labour in processing, cleaning, sorting, altering, finishing or packing articles. The work must be performed for gain or by way of trade. The Act does not cover most hotel and catering establishments with the exception of works canteens (attached to factories falling within the above definition) and food processing establishments.

The Act specifies minimum standards of protection, safety and welfare, in a similar way to the Office, Shops and Railway Premises Act.

YOUNG PERSONS AND WOMEN

Many statutes have been enacted in the past, which have been intended to protect groups of people from exploitation including their being obliged to work excessive hours. The main groups protected in this way are young persons and women.

YOUNG PERSONS

This term refers to persons aged fifteen or over, but under the age of eighteen. The regulations vary for the different groups within the definition of young persons, and for the type of undertaking in which young persons are employed. The principle Acts cover :

Shops, including most hotel and catering undertakings; Shops Act 1950 and the Young Persons (Employment) Acts 1938 and 1964.

Factories, including works canteens; Factories Act 1961.

Industrial undertakings other than factories; the Employment of Women, Young Persons' and Children's Act 1920.

These Acts are concerned primarily with protecting the physical well-being of young persons and with specifying the hours which they are permitted to work.

The regulations are quite detailed but can vary in detail from one part of the country to another as they are administered mainly by local authorities. Regulations cover the following points:

Hours of work
Hours on the employer's premises
Hours off duty
Frequency and duration of rest and meal breaks
Permitted overtime
Holidays
Medical examinations.

For details of the regulations as they apply to a particular area it is advisable to contact the local office of the department of employment.

WOMEN

Regulations covering the employment of women, with particular respect to the hotel and catering industry are few (apart from differences in the Wages Councils Instruments). The principle one affecting this industry along with many other industries, is as follows.

THE EQUAL PAY ACT 1970

The purpose of this Act is to remove differences in terms and conditions of employment between men and women employed on the same or very similar work. Equality of pay should be established by 29 December 1975. The onus of proof that any differences in pay result from reasons other than sex will rest with the employer. Industrial tribunals will deal with any complaints and will be able to award arrears of pay and damages. It is possible that job evaluation will play a critical part in determining pay differentials between jobs, once this Act becomes effective.

OTHER LEGISLATION

Apart from legislation concerned with contracts, pay and conditions of work there are several other important statutes concerned with various other aspects of employment, including the following.

SOCIAL SECURITY

The Social Security Scheme provides a wide variety of benefits and welfare services such as benefits for unemployment, sickness, industrial injuries and also retirement. Most people over school-leaving age and under pensionable age (65 for men, 60 for women) are insurable. Persons who are insurable must register and obtain a National Insurance number.

There are four classes of contribution for Social Security purposes : —

Class	I	Employed earners (which will include "office holders" such as Directors who may previously have been self-employed).
Class	II	Self-employed earners.
Class	III	Payable voluntarily by earners and others to secure basic scheme benefits not earned by payment of Class I and/or Class II.
Class	IV	Payable by self-employed earners whose profits or gains taxable under Schedule D are more than a certain figure.

As this book is intended primarily for those employing others, only Class I will be examined in any detail. The main regulations, after April, 1975, are : —

(1) An employer is responsible for paying the total contributions, although he can recover the employee's proportion from wages before they are paid.

(2) Contributions will be payable as a percentage of all earnings up to £69.00 per week provided they amount to at least £11.00 a week. The primary Class I (Employed Earners) contribution being 5.5% and the secondary Class I (Employers) contribution 8.5%.

(3) Class I contributions must be paid in respect of all separate employments from which earnings are at least £11.00 per week. Class II (and if appropriate Class IV) may also be payable at the same time. There is, however, a limit to the total amount payable.

(4) The contribution week runs from Saturday midnight to Saturday midnight; where the contribution week straddles two tax years it is regarded as being in the first.

(5) Liability for contributions will not depend on whether services are rendered but on whether earnings are paid.

Therefore, if an employee is incapacitated but is receiving pay of at least £11.00 per week contributions will be payable during that period.

(6) Retirement Pensioners are not liable to pay contributions when they work (they are, however, subject to an earnings rule). The Employer's contribution is nevertheless payable. Married women and certain widows may elect to pay a reduced contribution of 2%.

(7) Staff employed through an Agency should have their contributions paid by the agency.

(8) Contributions must be recorded on the deduction card supplied by the Inland Revenue and paid to Inland Revenue within fourteen days of the end of the Tax month.

Leaflets covering particular aspects of the Social Security scheme are usually available on demand from the Local Office of the Department of Health and Social Security.

EMPLOYER'S LIABILITY

Every employer has a liability to insure against injury or disease suffered by his employees in the course of the employers' business. (Employers' Liability (Compulsory Insurance) Act 1969.)

REDUNDANCY PAYMENTS ACTS 1965 & 1969

These Acts provide for compensation to those persons who have been employed continuously by one employer for 104 weeks or more, who are normally employed for twenty-one hours or more per week and who have been dismissed because their jobs have been eliminated due to the need for their particular work having declined or ceased.

The employer can offer alternative employment but it must be reasonable in relation to the employee's previous work. If an employee refuses a reasonable alternative he will forfeit his right to a redundancy payment.

Men in their sixty-fourth year (fifty-ninth for women) who have been made redundant have any entitlement to redundancy reduced by one-twelfth for each month of service following their sixty-fourth birthday (fifty-ninth for women). Where occupational pension

Fig.45 Redundancy payment calculation

For each year of service in a particular age range an employee qualifies for ½, 1 or 1½ weeks' pay.
This is as follows:

   18 years to 21 years ½ week's pay
   22 years to 40 years 1 week's pay
   41 years to 65 years 1½ weeks' pay
   (women 60 yrs)

A maximum of 20 years' service is allowed with a maximum week's pay of £40; the maximum payment is therefore £1,200.

The number of years' service is calculated by working from the time of redundancy backwards thus giving the maximum benefit.

schemes are in operation an employer's obligations may be modified. The redundancy payments are calculated as shown in figure 45.

The employer contributes to the Redundancy Payment Fund through a charge on the National Insurance stamp and he qualifies for a fifty per cent rebate on any redundancy payments that he may make to redundant employees. Notice that a claim is likely to be made must be given to the local office of the Department of Employment before a person is made redundant.

RACE RELATIONS ACT 1968

The Race Relations Act makes it illegal to discriminate against anyone employed or seeking employment on the grounds of colour, race, ethnic or national origin.

Discrimination is only permitted if it is done in order to ensure a reasonable balance between different groups. It is also permissible to employ persons of particular nationalities because they have certain skills, or other qualifications. This is very relevant to the hotel and catering industry where frequently only people of a particular nationality will have the necessary knowledge, skills or languages to work in a restaurant specialising in a particular nation's dishes. Advertisements however should specify the skills and knowledge required and not nationality.

THE DISABLED PERSONS (EMPLOYMENT) ACTS 1944 & 1958

These Acts oblige employers of not less than twenty persons to employ a quota (currently three per cent) of disabled persons. Certain jobs are designated as suitable for disabled persons, and consequently these should be filled only by registered disabled persons. However employers may apply for a permit allowing them to employ less than their quota if they feel that their circumstances justify this.

INDUSTRIAL TRAINING ACT 1964

The Industrial Training Act became law in order to stimulate industrial training and to spread the cost evenly over most employers in an industry. To do this industrial training boards were established.

The Hotel and Catering Industry Training Board is the board with responsibilities for all hotel and catering training matters, and in order to finance its activities it charges the industry's employers a levy. The levy in 1974 was 0.7 per cent of payroll, with employers having a payroll of less than £30,000 per annum being exempted.

The levy is reduced or waived, for those employers liable to pay it, if they have planned and approved training programmes.

The Board provides advisory services and assists in the running of group training schemes.

EMPLOYMENT OF FOREIGN LABOUR

Within the hotel and catering industry foreign workers represent a substantial proportion of the total work force. The main regulations covering the employment of foreigners are :

E.E.C. NATIONALS

No permits are required because E.E.C. nationals are free to seek employment in any E.E.C. country. After three months an E.E.C. national is entitled to a residence permit in the country in which he is employed.

COMMONWEALTH CITIZENS AND ALIENS

The employment of commonwealth citizens (who are not patrials) and aliens is strictly controlled and a quota system regulating the total number of such employees is operated. They must be in possession of work permits when coming to the U.K. to work.

APPLICATIONS FOR PERMITS

Applications for permits have to be made to the Department of Employment and these require documentary evidence from previous employers that the prospective employee has the minimum necessary experience as laid down by the Department of Employment. The experience required varies for different jobs, the minimum being one year for still-room maids and the maximum five years for cooks, waiters and management. Age limits are laid down for different jobs with a maximum of fifty-four in all cases.

As these requirements can change from year to year, and as several countries have regulations regarding their own nationals working abroad, it is advisable always to obtain the most up-to-date information regarding the employment of foreigners beforehand. The B.H.R.C.A. (see Appendix 1) and the Department of Employment can be of assistance.

THE INDUSTRIAL RELATIONS ACT

This major statute for the first time brought together a great deal of related law concerned with many different aspects of employment. It was based on the principles that :

Collective bargaining must be conducted responsibly. Orderly procedures for settling disputes must be maintained – at the same time providing safeguards for the community. Employees and employers have the right to join associations of workers or of employers, as appropriate. Individuals are protected against unfair industrial practices.

The major provisions of this Act follow :

RIGHTS OF INDIVIDUALS

Rights of individuals were created allowing a man to belong or not to belong to a trade union and also granting protection against 'unfair dismissal'.

UNFAIR INDUSTRIAL PRACTICES

A new concept in our law was created, the 'unfair industrial practice', which included a variety of actions such as threatening industrial action in order to induce an employer to dismiss an employee unfairly.

NEW INSTITUTIONS

Four important new institutions were created to help the conduct of Industrial Relations. These were the National Industrial Relations Court, the Commission on Industrial Relations, the Industrial Arbitration Board and the Industrial Tribunals.

TRADE UNION RECOGNITION

New methods by which trade union disputes and their bargaining rights could be determined were introduced. These included, in particular, agency shops and the secret ballot.

COOLING OFF PERIOD

Protection for the community in an emergency was provided for by the Secretary of State having the right to apply to the Industrial Court for a 'cooling off' period.

So far as the Hotel and Catering industry is concerned probably the most important provision, at this time, is the one affording protection to employees against 'unfair' dismissal. In time, other sections of this Act or any Acts that replace it will increase in importance particularly that covering trade union bargaining rights.

TRADE UNION AND LABOUR RELATIONS BILL

The Industrial Relations Act, in some respects, proved to be unsatisfactory, with the consequence that the Trade Union and Labour Relations Bill was placed before Parliament in the Spring of 1974. It was designed to repeal the Industrial Relations Act – at the same time re-enacting, with certain changes, some provisions of that Act and, in particular, those relating to unfair dismissal. It was also designed to abolish the National Industrial Relations Court, the Commission on Industrial Relations and the Registry of Trade Unions and Employers' Associations.

The Bill defines a trade union as an organisation which

"consists wholly or mainly of workers of one or more descriptions and is an organisation whose principal purposes include the regulation of relations between workers of that description or those descriptions and employers or employers' associations".

The status of trade unions is defined with the result that, only in certain cases can a trade union be treated as a 'body corporate'.

An employers' association is defined and may be either a 'body corporate' or an unincorporated association.

Immunities from actions in tort are provided for, for those acts done in contemplation or furtherance of a trade dispute, so that those who induce or threaten to induce another person to break a contract or to interfere with its performance cannot be sued. This protection extends to trade unions, employers' associations, their members and officials and also to those conspiring to carry out such acts.

Picketing is lawful, so long as it is confined to 'peacefully obtaining or communicating information, or peacefully persuading any person to work or abstain from work', and is not carried out at his place of residence.

The position regarding legal enforceability of collective agreements is that they will only be legally enforceable if the agreement specifically provides that it is intended to be legally enforceable. Furthermore, any terms in collective agreements restricting workers from engaging in industrial action shall not form part of a contract unless the collective agreement : —

a) is in writing and states that those terms may be incorporated in such a contract

b) is reasonably accessible

c) is one where the trade unions concerned are independent trade unions.

A major change from the Industrial Relations Act, and one which is intended to recognise industrial realities, is that 'closed shops' are permitted, where a union and an employer have entered into a union membership agreement.

The consequence of this provision is that it is fair to dismiss an employee who refused to become or remain a member of a specified independent trade union with which the employer had entered into a union membership agreement.

These summaries are very brief and only pick out the major features of what are probably the most relevant legislation to employers in the hotel and catering industry. Because of their brevity these summaries cannot be authoritative and where a particular point of law is in question the Act itself should be studied, or a lawyer consulted. However, for those who have a constant need to refer to employment legislation there is an admirable work in loose leaf form which is constantly up-dated by the publisher. This is Croner's *Reference Book for Employers*.

FURTHER READING

Pollard, W. B. (ed.), *Reference Book for Employers,* Croner, London, 1964.

Rose, F. W. *Personnel Management Law,* Gower Press, London, 1972.

16 Manpower planning, records and statistics

In recent years the importance of an undertaking's manpower resources has become much more apparent owing to the considerable costs of labour and the growing staff shortages in some sectors of the hotel and catering industry. In many other industries and organisations these problems have led to considerable attention being paid to most aspects of man management. It has led, in particular, to accurate manpower planning so that an employer has the right resources available when required and also so that labour costs are not unnecessarily high. Because of this, well conceived personnel policies are now playing an increasingly important part in furthering many undertakings' business objectives. They translate the overall business plan into a detailed manpower plan. Sound personnel policies can only be achieved through a thorough understanding of the organisation, its objectives, its management, its operating style, and its social and political environment.

Personnel policies must play a positive and creative role in the plans, developments and day-to-day activities of an undertaking. They must be designed to provide competent manpower resources when required. The need to plan on a sound basis of reliable information has been emphasised and much of a manager's work revolves around certain basic and fundamental information. For example the need for precise job descriptions has been shown to be vital not only to recruitment, but also to training, performance appraisal, job evaluation and salary administration.

Manpower planning is divided into two separate and distinct parts : operational and strategic. Operational is concerned with the day-to-day manning problems of an organisation such as the filling of vacancies caused by staff leaving. The strategic part of manpower is concerned with ensuring that the right manpower will be available in the longer term, for example for hotels that are not even built.

At the operational level management needs to know precisely what manning ratios are necessary. Each company and each establishment will have its own, such as one waiter for ten covers and one chambermaid for twelve rooms.

At the strategic level management needs accurate manpower statistics in order to develop the undertaking's long-term plans. This is best illustrated by an example. If, for instance, a brewery company wanted to expand its number of managed public houses by 100 it would need to recruit at least 100 new husband and wife teams to run these public houses. In addition if it had 100 managed houses already it would have to anticipate finding replacements for some of these existing 100 managers. If wastage rates are unknown it is not possible to calculate accurately what numbers to recruit and train. On the other hand if the company has kept records these may show that wastage amongst established managers is twenty per cent per annum and among trainees it is thirty per cent. It is then simple to determine how many to recruit in a year.

As 100 couples are required for new houses and twenty couples are required for existing houses, this indicates that a total of 120 couples are needed to complete training. However, as wastage during training is thirty per cent the number to be recruited will have to be increased to compensate for this loss.

$$\text{Thus}: \frac{120 \times 100}{70} = 172 \text{ couples (rounded up)}.$$

This then is the number needed for training.

The brewery therefore knows on the basis of past experience that it will need to recruit about 172 couples to fill 120 vacancies likely to occur in the next year. The actual phasing of this recruitment depends on other factors such as the length of training, the availability of new public houses, the policy for retiring or replacing tenants, etc. This illustrates that plans for the future are difficult to implement effectively without adequate records and statistics.

However, as was said much earlier, the individual's needs, as well as the employer's, have to be recognised – consequently any records and statistical data must serve the individual as well as the employer.

Personnel information and records are required for several reasons :

1. To provide detailed operational information such as monthly strength returns and payroll analyses.

2. To provide ratios or data such as wastage rates, age analyses and service analyses for planning purposes.

3. To provide information on individuals for administration purposes such as salaries and pensions and to provide information for career development purposes.

4. To provide information for statutory purposes such as National Insurance, Redundancy Payment or Registered Disabled Persons Act.

5. To provide information for re-employment and reference purposes.

The nature of records and statistics that may be maintained and produced by employers varies considerably. The largest organisations in this country will require highly sophisticated information possibly using computer based systems, whereas smaller organisations will need only minimal information. However, the following are probably basic to most organisations employing more than a few people.

PERSONAL RECORD

This is the backbone of a good records system. If both the contents and the layout are designed carefully it can provide valuable information quickly and easily. Whether this record is a simple index card, a visible edge card, a punch card or on a computer file, depends on the number of employees and the amount of detail required. Generally speaking, a visible edge card is quite adequate for most employers, small or large. For the few employers with several thousand people punched cards using machine sorting, or even computer based systems will probably be more appropriate.

The card should be a record containing concise information which will be common to most employees such as age, education, qualifications, training, marital status. It is used primarily for statistical exercises or for the speedy retrieval of information. For example the personal record cards may be used to produce an age distribution of all management employees in order to assist with management development plans, or alternatively the cards may be used to discover French speakers or all those with 'instructor' training. The personal record card does not replace the need for a personal dossier for each employee.

A typical personal record card will look like the one shown in figure 46.

Fig.46 A personal record card

Address							Tel No.
Change							Tel No.
Next of kin							
Address		Relationship					Tel No.

PREVIOUS EMPLOYMENT

Firm	Address	Occupation	From	To	Why left

EDUCATION

From	To	Place	Qualifications

PRESENT EMPLOYMENT

Date	Job/Branch	Grade	Rate	Report

TRAINING

Date	Course	Result

MEDICAL HISTORY	GENERAL REMARKS

Date left	Reason for leaving

No.	Surname	Christian name(s)	Date of birth	Occ.	Date commenced	Loc.	Absent			
							Hol.	Sick	W'out leave	P.

PERSONAL DOSSIER

This should contain all documents relating to an individual
employee. These may include :

   Copies of letters of offer and acceptance
   Application form
   Copy of engagement form
   Various reports and correspondence
   Performance appraisals
   Changes of conditions, e.g. salary increases
   Records of company property issued to the employee.

The dossier is usually kept for a period of time (a year or two) after
an employee has left, in case of queries.

EMPLOYMENT REQUISITION

This is a document produced by the heads of departments (in larger
organisations) requesting authority to recruit a replacement or an
addition to staff. The nature of this form will vary considerably
and will depend on the degree of authority of individual heads of
departments. In some cases for example heads of departments will
need no special authority so long as the person to be recruited will
be within the laid down staff establishment or within authorised
budget levels. On the other hand, there are chief executives even
in some large organisations who insist on personally authorising

Fig.47 Example of an employment requisition

Splendide Hotel
REQUEST TO RECRUIT

Job   Dept   Grade   Wage

Replacement/increase to staff establishment *delete one*

Reason:

Requested by   Position   Date

Approved by personnel dept   Date

Authorised by   Date the recruitment of all new staff whether they are replacing leavers or exceeding the staff establishment.

In most of the larger well-organised undertakings, the personnel department will also have to authorise the salary or wage to be paid in order to ensure that anomalies are not allowed to creep in.

A typical form is shown in figure 47.

ENGAGEMENT FORM

This form should be completed when a new employee joins an employer. The purpose is to inform all the relevant departments so that appropriate action is initiated. These departments may include :

> Wages
> Training
> Pensions
> Insurance
> Personnel Records.

The information contained on the form will vary according to the system being used. For example some employers may be able to use one engagement form for all departments and all levels of staff whereas other employers may need to use different forms for each. It is of prime importance, however, to ensure that the employee is paid and insured. Consequently information will have to include name, staff number, address, department, date of starting, rate of pay, bank address. Figure 48 shows one typical example.

TERMINATION FORM

This form is necessary in order to fulfil several purposes :

1. To initiate documentation and administration procedures such as the preparation of the P45, the National Insurance cards, the final wages payment.
2. To provide statistical information regarding labour turnover.
3. To provide information for reference or re-employment purposes.

OTHER FORMS

There is a variety of other information that may have to be kept for statutory or other purposes. These can include :

Fig.48 Example of an Engagement Form

S *Splendide Hotel, Newtown,*
Newtownshire.
Tel.: Newtown (0021) 12345

Surname	Other names	Staff no
Address	National Insurance No	Job
		Department
Telephone	RDP Number	Branch

Next of kin *to be notified in case of accident*

Name   Telephone No
Address

Date commenced

Hours and days of duty

Rate of pay

Service charge percentage

Method and frequency of payment

Bank address

P45 received   YES/NO

Insurance cards received   YES/NO

Special comments *such as holiday arrangements to be honoured*

Copies sent to:	Wages	Pensions/insurance
	Personnel	Head of department

Completed by   Position   Date

Accident reports
Medical reports
Training reports
Absentee reports
Change of status, e.g. salary increases, promotions, transfers
Warnings.

From these various documents the majority of statistical information required for the satisfactory planning and control of most undertakings can be produced. This information may include the following :

STRENGTH RETURNS

This will show numbers employed by departments and should show changes in numbers. It may also incorporate 'establishment' numbers, that is the agreed numbers to be employed in each department. Any variation from 'establishment' will be shown.

PAYROLL ANALYSIS

This information (a development of the strength return) may be produced by a variety of departments including the wages department, and the cost or management accountant's department, or the personnel manager's department. It will include a breakdown, by departments, of labour costs. These may be shown in a large variety of ways including various ratios and percentages. The figures should always include a comparison of the actual and budget figures.

Both the strength return and the payroll analysis should be produced on a regular periodic basis. Where there is strict control over wage and salary levels the 'strength return' will be sufficient for most day-to-day management purposes, since cost variances will only arise where there are variances from the laid down 'establishment'. In any case the labour costs should show up elsewhere – in particular on periodic operating statements.

STAFF/LABOUR TURNOVER ANALYSIS

This has already been examined in Chapter 13 on Termination of Employment. However, it must be stressed that the regular production of this information can assist considerably in staff recruitment and retention by identifying the problem areas.

The turnover rate for each department and for the undertaking as a whole will make up part of this report. This can be arrived at roughly by the following formula :

$$\frac{Number\ of\ employees\ who\ left\ during\ period \times 100}{Average\ number\ employed\ during\ period}$$

In itself the turnover rate may be of little value as it gives no indication, for example, of turnover among long-serving employees. It may, therefore, be necessary to supplement labour turnover figures with further breakdowns. This may be done in a variety of ways including showing numbers of leavers by length of service as shown in figure 49.

Fig.49 An analysis of 'leavers' by length of service

ANALYSIS OF LEAVERS FOR 12 MONTHS ENDING 31 DECEMBER 1973

Length of service	Number of leavers	Percentage
Years		
more than 5	4	5.0%
more than 2 less than 5	8	10.0%
more than 1 less than 2	10	12.5%
up to 1	58	72.5%
TOTAL	80	100.0%

AGE AND SERVICE ANALYSES

For manpower planning and management development purposes it is important in the medium and larger-sized organisations from time to time to look at the make-up of the labour force and in particular at the age profile of the management team. If this is not done an unanticipated spate of retirements and resignations can leave an undertaking without the necessary trained personnel. It is useful, therefore, to produce an annual age profile of management, headed by those due to retire. In some cases it may be desirable to link this with service and this can be done easily in this way (see figure 50).

In examining the type of chart shown in figure 50 one would hope to see the bulk of managers distributed fairly evenly through the chart preferably with a slightly greater weight at the younger end. Where this is not the case the management team may not have the necessary combination of age, experience and inbuilt continuity. Consequently senior management may wish to take steps to put this right by promotion, transfers, recruitment and appropriate training.

Fig.50 An age and service analysis

SERVICE

Age	under 1 year	$\frac{1}{5}$	$\frac{6}{10}$	$\frac{11}{15}$	$\frac{16}{20}$	$\frac{21}{25}$	$\frac{26}{30}$	$\frac{31}{35}$	$\frac{36}{40}$	41 +
$\frac{61}{65}$			1		2		2			
$\frac{56}{60}$						1				
$\frac{51}{55}$		6	3	3		1				
$\frac{46}{50}$	3		2							
$\frac{41}{45}$	1									
$\frac{36}{40}$			1	1	2					
$\frac{31}{35}$	2	8	1							
$\frac{26}{30}$	8	7								
$\frac{21}{25}$	2	3								
under 21	1	2								

MANPOWER AUDIT

Some of the largest employers conduct detailed studies periodically which provide a complete breakdown of the labour force divided into various sections including job grades, age and service. They may also report on the quality of staff, their qualifications, performance and potential. The training plan, management development programme and manpower plan may be part of, or may be linked with, this audit.

Apart from the records and data discussed here there are many more that may be necessary for effective planning and control. However it is important to bear in mind that although the production of information and statistics, in itself, can be an attractive occupation only those data that serve a useful purpose must be produced. They should clearly be aids to line management in providing an effective service. If they do not satisfy this requirement the information being produced is almost certainly unwanted and consequently it is a waste of resources that could be employed more fruitfully elsewhere.

FURTHER READING

Kelly, T., *Personnel Records and Manpower Planning*, HCITB, London, 1971.

Appendix 1

STAFF RECRUITMENT ORGANISATIONS

The following organisations can be of assistance in recruiting staff.

Department of Employment. The Department of Employment now operates over twenty branches which specialise in hotel and catering staff. The address and telephone number of the nearest such branch can be obtained from the local office of the Department of Employment.

In addition the Department runs a specialised hotel and catering staff service at:

1–3 Denmark St
London WC2H 8LR
Telephone 01–836–6622

Employment Agencies. The Federation of Personnel Services of Great Britain is the principle association of employment agencies in Great Britain. The Federation lays down a code of conduct to which members agree to conform. The names, addresses and telephone numbers of member firms in any given area can be obtained by telephoning the Federation. The Federation's address is: The Federation of Personnel Services of Great Britain, 120 Baker St, London W1M 2DE. *Telephone* 01–487–5250, 01–487–5273.

Management Consultants. There are several management consultancy firms that can be of assistance in recruiting staff of middle

and senior management positions. The names of such firms can
be obtained from :

British Institute of Management
Management House
Parker St
London WC2B 5PT
Telephone 01–405–3456

Hotel Catering and Institutional Management Association
191 Trinity Rd
London SW17 7HN
Telephone 01–672–4251

Management Consultants Association
23–24 Cromwell Place
London SW7 2LG
Telephone 01–584–7283

Recruitment of overseas workers. Queries regarding the recruitment of foreign staff should be directed to :

the local office of the Department of Employment

or to

Department of Employment
Training Services Agency
Ebury Bridge House
Ebury Bridge Rd
London SWW 8PY
Telephone 01–730–9661

or to

The British Hotel, Restaurants and Caterers' Association
20 Upper Brook St
London W1Y 2BH
Telephone 01–499–6641

Appendix 2

TRAINING ORGANISATIONS

The following organisations can be of assistance in providing advice, training materials or courses for the training of staff or management :

Trade/Official bodies

British Association for Commercial and Industrial
  Education
16 Park Crescent
London W1N 4AP
Telephone 01–636–5351

British Institute of Management
Management House
Parker St
London WC2B 5PT
Telephone 01–405–3456

Hotel and Catering Industry Training Board
P.O. Box 18
Ramsey House
Central Square
Wembley
Middlesex HA9 7AP
Telephone 01–902–8865

Industrial Society
P.O. Box 1 BQ
Robert Hyde House
48 Bryanston Square
London W1A 1BQ
Telephone 01–262–2401

Management Consultants

Cornwell Greene Bertram Smith & Co.
20 Kingsway
London WC2B 6LH
Telephone 01–405–3861

HCS (Management Consultants) Ltd
4 Station Parade
Eastbourne
Sussex BN21 1BE
Telephone Eastbourne 20615

The names of additional firms of management consultants can be obtained from :

British Institute of Management
Management House
Parker St
London WC2B 5PT
Telephone 01–405–3456

Hotel Catering and Institutional Management Association
191 Trinity Rd
London SW17 7HN
Telephone 01–672–4251

Management Consultants Association
23–24 Cromwell Place
London SW7 2LG
Telephone 01–584–7283

Directories of Courses

Directory of Courses
30 High St
Kingston-upon-Thames
Surrey KT1 1HL
Telephone 01–549–2256

Management Courses Index
Haymarket Publishing Ltd
Gillow House
5 Winsley St
London W1A 2HG
Telephone 01–636–3600

Appendix 3

SALARY ADMINISTRATION AND JOB EVALUATION
The following organisations can be of assistance in job evaluation
and salary administration :
Professional bodies
    British Institute of Management
    Management House
    Parker St
    London WC2B 5PT
    Telephone 01-405-3456
    Hotel Catering and Institutional Management Association
    191 Trinity Rd
    London SW17 7HN
    Telephone 01-672-4251
    Institute of Administrative Management
    205 High Street
    Beckenham
    Kent BR3 1BA
    Telephone 01-658-0171
    Institute of Personnel Management
    5 Winsley St
    Oxford Circus
    London W1N 7AQ
    Telephone 01-580-3271

Management Consultants Association
23–24 Cromwell Place
London SW7 2LG
Telephone 01–584–7283

Management Consultants

The following organisations specialise in the hotel and catering industry:

Cornwell Greene Bertram Smith & Co.
20 Kingsway
London WC2B 6LH
Telephone 01–405–3861

HCS (Management Consultants) Ltd
4 Station Parade
Eastbourne
Sussex BN21 1BE
Telephone Eastbourne 20615

The names of additional firms can be obtained from:

British Institute of Management
Management House
Parker St
London WC2B 5PT
Telephone 01–405–3456

Management Consultants Association
23–24 Cromwell Place
London SW7 2LG
Telephone 01–584–7283

Salary advice, Surveys and information bureaux

Alfred Marks Bureau Ltd
8–9 Frith St
London W1R 1RF
Telephone 01–437–7855

Management Survey Centre
30 High St
Kingston-upon-Thames
Surrey KT1 1HL
Telephone 01–549–2256

Institute of Administrative Management
205 High St
Beckenham
Kent BR3 1BA
Telephone 01–658–0171

Index